# CYCLING CLIMBS OF SOUTH-WEST ENGLAND

## A ROAD CYCLIST'S GUIDE

GW00669812

**F**

FRANCES
LINCOLN

Frances Lincoln Limited
A subsidiary of Quarto Publishing Group UK
74–77 White Lion Street
London N1 9PF

Cycling Climbs of South-West England: A Road Cyclist's Guide

First Frances Lincoln edition 2017

A catalogue record for this book is available from the British Library.

978-0-7112-3707-0

Printed and bound in China

1 2 3 4 5 6 7 8 9

Quarto is the authority on a wide range of topics.

Quarto educates, entertains and enriches the lives of
our readers – enthusiasts and lovers of hands-on living.

www.QuartoKnows.com

MIX
Paper from
responsible sources
FSC® C016973

Thanks to my family and friends for their continued support
and patience while I continue to disappear for days on end searching
out hills. Thanks to all the Strava users and my Twitter followers who have
suggested climbs for me to seek out, and thanks to whoever was in
charge of the weather in the spring of 2016. I really appreciated
riding in the pouring rain just about every day.

# CONTENTS

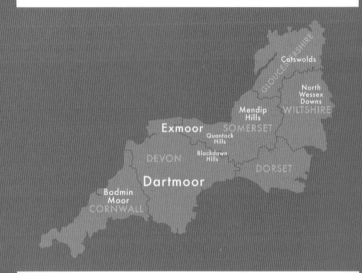

# THE SOUTH-WEST

I spent a fair amount of time in unknown territory while compiling this book. Although I'd ridden around Somerset and covered plenty of the roads around Dartmoor, Exmoor and into Cornwall, I'd almost entirely bypassed Wiltshire and Dorset on my travels, so I went to make amends. I began my research, however, on a trip to compete in the annual Minehead CC race up the Porlock Toll Road. I'd read about this climb but never ridden it, put off by the prospect of paying the £1 toll, no doubt. But what an amazing road it is, and what a fantastic event; an instant classic, from the Tour de France-style start ramp in front of the hordes of fans to the sheer joy of snaking up through the woods on a pristine strip of snaking, traffic-free tarmac. The majority of hill climb races in Britain are run up short, savage climbs so it's great to find

Tejvan Pettinger on the start ramp of the 2015 Minehead CC hill climb on the Porlock Toll Road.

one that uses a longer, steadier incline more akin to the great Alpine passes (although about 10 kilometres shorter). I will be coming back again and again to this event. I followed the race with an afternoon warm-down criss-crossing the Mendip Hills, which is a brilliant place to ride if you want to pack a multitude of climbs into a short distance – including, of course, the wonderful Cheddar Gorge.

The next trip was to the Cotswolds to cover some familiar ground, tracing a route from Chipping Campden down to Stroud and back. I've done various interpretations of this ride over the past few years and have always managed to tackle a completely different sequence of climbs in the process – such is the variety of slopes. With Gloucestershire and Somerset covered, it was time to venture into Wiltshire and Dorset. Wiltshire doesn't have quite as much

to shout about, and it takes a little more looking to find that killer hill, but there are a few real gems, such as Bowden Hill and Fovant Downs, both of which will sting the legs.

Then it was on to Dorset. Wow, it's pretty: such beautiful villages, and so calm and quiet, just ideal for bike riding. I say this despite the fact that it was bucketing it down with rain almost every time I visited… I have no problem with riding in the rain, it's just the faff of having my camera, maps, phone etc all wrapped up in a multitude of ziplock bags. Of endlessly trying to keep the camera dry and the lens clean with permanently wet hands, and of course cleaning the bike at the end of each day!

I finished my research crossing Devon and Cornwall, where the choice of hills is simply bewildering. Between Exeter and Penzance there just isn't a flat

road, not one, so hard luck if you don't like hills, but great news if you do! All the way across Dartmoor, Bodmin Moor and down to Land's End is a climber's paradise, especially Cornwall where just about every coastal village lies at the base of a brutal little road. And they all follow the same routine: plummet down from the cliffs above to a peaceful harbour, turn right round, and then smash your legs on the way back up. Two of my very favourites are Talland Hill (page 162) and one I discovered for this book, Grove Road in St Mawes (page 164). Having made the long journey to find this climb, hidden as it is at the very tip of a tiny peninsula, I was determined to try and post a fast time online. I rode it once to check it out then rolled back down for a second attempt. However, halfway back up and well into the 'pain cave', I was confronted by a

group of tourists wobbling back from an afternoon's drinking. My tortured face and laboured breathing must have been quite a sobering sight as I lurched through them, unable to divert from my line, determined not to slow in my quest for a shot at the KOM on Strava!

After another four days of almost constant rain through Devon and Cornwall, at last the sun came out for my final research ride, and what a ride – and what climbs I found! I started with the vicious slopes of Grasspark Hill then finished with the twin climbs of Martinhoe Common and Trentishoe Down, both of which became instant favourites. I loved these roads: the way they wound through the forest, totally consumed by nature. I urge you to seek out these climbs – in fact, all of the climbs in this book – each of which has something truly special to offer.

# TOP OF THE WORLD

Although not quite as rare as hens' teeth, high points accessible by bike that offer uninterrupted 360-degree panoramic views are quite rare. If you search hard enough though, and you're ready to put in some serious work to reach them, there are a handful of peaks dotted around Britain that genuinely do give you that on-top-of-the-world feeling. Plateaus where there's nothing between you and the sky, allowing you to survey the entirety of the surrounding landscape for as far as your eyes (or more likely the weather conditions) will allow. Standing on top of one of these summits on a clear day, with the endorphins flowing and the legs screaming from the effort to get there, is pure heaven, and no matter how pressing your schedule it will force a timeout. They demand a halt to your ride, insisting you take the opportunity to put your life into perspective as you look out into the distance. Although the views may fall slightly short of those from, say, the International Space Station or the peerless Mont Ventoux in France, they are truly special places and must be relished.

So how do you find them? Well, first of all, I've handily documented many throughout my series of climbing guides, from Great Dunn Fell in the Pennines down to Kit Hill (page 156). Some have reputations that precede them, others take a little more searching, but there are a couple of icons on the OS Landranger maps that are there to help: the mast icon (below) and the 360 viewpoint icon (see overleaf).

Firstly, the mast icon – this little obtuse triangle with bolts of lightning emanating from the spire is a surefire sign of certain vertical ascent and potential pain, but be warned, they aren't all accessible by bike and the majority lie well off the beaten track. When building a transmitter mast it is essential to find the highest available plot close to your desired location, ideally one that has a clean line of sight in all directions. Then you'll need to transport the necessary materials up to construct it and in future maintain it, and for this you want a proper access road. Unfortunately most sit at the top of neglected old dirt roads, which to us are useless. In a few special cases though a bespoke strip of asphalt has been laid, reserved for official vehicles and yes, of course, us cyclists. These roads often have a gate at the bottom to stop unauthorised entry but I've yet to find one that isn't open to riders and walkers. Naturally these climbs are quiet, very quiet – and often steep, very steep! A little used service road doesn't need to pander to the needs of everyday traffic so there's no need for a series of lacets or a complex tangle of hairpin bends – if you can get a 4x4 up it in a straight line then there's no point in wasting tarmac, right?

The second special icon is the viewpoint icon. OS Landranger maps are covered with the standard semicircle of cyan triangles along coastlines and cliffs, indicating a spectacular lookout, but what I'm interested in are the complete circles like the one below. These spots offer the full monty: an uninterrupted sweep of the world around in all directions.

I've spent hours scanning maps for these magic marks, looking for congested contours with the proverbial cherry on top. For those of us seeking out a killer climb with a killer view, these are the signals that widen our eyes and have us scrambling out of the door. Unlike the service roads up to transmitter masts, the high points marked with viewpoint logos will usually have much better public access, but the roads will also be slightly more congested as a result.

Of the handful of these special roads I have thus far ridden and documented here are three that really stand out. Firstly Great Dunn Fell. I have likened this to the aforementioned Mont Ventoux thanks to its spectacular height, and just like the giant French mountain it's prone to hostile weather at the top. One minor drawback to this summit is that the giant radar station slightly spoils the uninterrupted views, but only slightly. For the ultimate in 360-degree vistas you may not find better than Abdon Burf on Brown Clee Hill in Shropshire (found in *Cycling Climbs of the Midlands*). Once you've recovered from its hideously tough ascent, dismount and make the very short walk to the small monument on the summit, climb on top (which isn't easy in cycling shoes) and enjoy. I love this place – no matter how much it hurts to get there, the views of the flowing Shropshire hills are just magnificent.

And thirdly, in this volume, the climb up to Kit Hill (page 156) also blew me away. The route up from Luckett is brutal to say the least: a seemingly endless 20% ramp in and out of the woods before a stunning finale. As soon as you make the right turn up the tiny road to the peak, you know you're in for a treat. At the summit lies an old mine chimney, a brick obelisk that's been your focus for the entirety of your ride. And again, like Abdon Burf, this spot allows you to see for miles and miles in all directions.

So go seek out these roads and divert your rides for the chance to reach the ultimate elevation. Once you're at the summit sit back and enjoy being on top of the world.

**REMEMBER**
to check
your bike, check
your body, wear
a helmet, and, above
all, have fun!

# LEGEND

## LOCATIONS

You will be able to locate each hill from the small maps provided: simply, **S** marks the start and **F** marks the finish. I would suggest you invest in either Ordnance Survey maps or a GPS system to help plan your routes in more detail. The grid reference in the Factfile locates the summit of each climb, and in brackets is the relevant **OS Landranger** map. The graphic at the start of each chapter will show you where the hills lie in the context of each region.

## TIMINGS

Each Factfile includes the approximate time needed to ride each hill. Timed over the distance marked, this is how long it took me to complete each climb at a reasonable, but comfortable pace. Since I rode in all weathers, from blizzards to baking heat, I have adjusted the times slightly to accommodate for the adverse conditions I faced on the day. The times could be used as a target but are really just intended to help you plan your rides.

## FACTFILE

**WHERE** If you are riding along the A370, leave it in Flax Bourton and head north to join the B3130 where you head straight across to climb.

| | |
|---|---|
| **GRID REF** | ST 525 715 (OS172) |
| **LENGTH** | 2200m |
| **HEIGHT GAIN** | 113m |
| **APPROX CLIMB TIME** | 5 mins |

## RATINGS

The climbs are rated from **1/10** to **10/10** within the context of the book. The rating is an amalgamation of gradient, length, the likely hostility of the riding conditions, and the condition of the surface. All the climbs are tough, therefore **1/10** equals 'hard', and **10/10** equals 'it's all you can do to keep your bike moving'. Some will suit you more than others; the saying 'horses for courses' applies, but all the **10/10** climbs will test any rider.

## MAP KEY

| | |
|---|---|
| Motorway | M1 |
| **A** Road | A123 |
| **B** Road | B1234 |
| Minor Road | |
| Rail line | STATION |
| Hill route | S START — F FINISH |
| Town | TOWN |
| Scale | 2km |

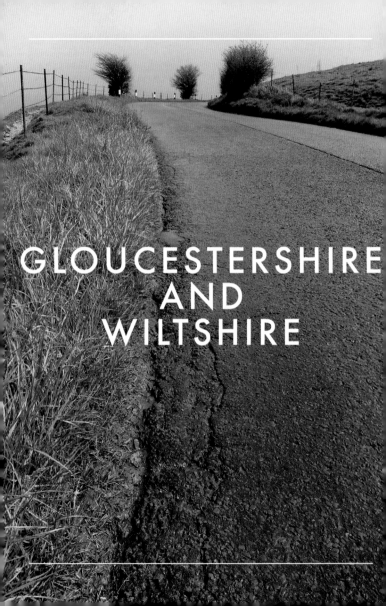

GLOUCESTERSHIRE
AND
WILTSHIRE

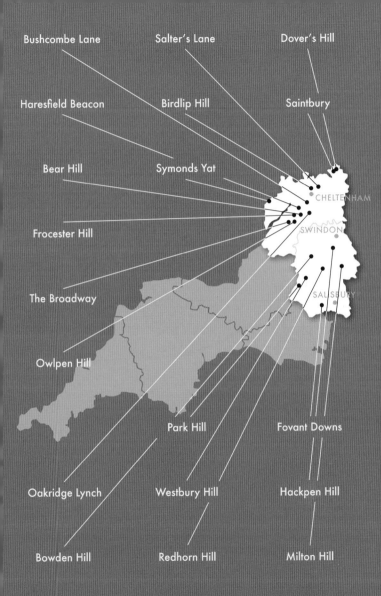

Bushcombe Lane

Salter's Lane

Dover's Hill

Haresfield Beacon

Birdlip Hill

Saintbury

Bear Hill

Symonds Yat

CHELTENHAM

Frocester Hill

SWINDON

The Broadway

Owlpen Hill

SALISBURY

Park Hill

Fovant Downs

Oakridge Lynch

Westbury Hill

Hackpen Hill

Bowden Hill

Redhorn Hill

Milton Hill

# DOVER'S HILL

Deep in the beautiful Cotswolds, this little road has been used for numerous National Hill Climb Championships. It's not the sharpest of climbs – its popularity probably lies in its central location and pleasant surroundings, and it's one of a number of decent hills in the area. Start your climb from Weston-sub-Edge and head south up the ridge, passing the church and the picture-postcard stone houses lining the road rising out of the village. Dotted with drainage grilles, the road kinks left then climbs harder up to a sharp right into a tunnel created by the overhanging canopy of branches. The road surface is rough under the trees, but the climb never becomes too extreme, with a maximum 14% gradient. The topping continues to deteriorate as the road gradually arcs left, leaving the woods behind as it nears the summit. The now-lumpy tarmac re-enters tree cover as the gradient ebbs towards the crest at the Dover's Hill car park.

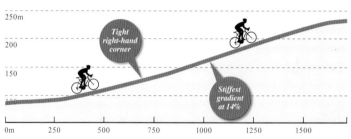

Tight right-hand corner

Stiffest gradient at 14%

250m
200
150

0m    250    500    750    1000    1250    1500

## FACTFILE

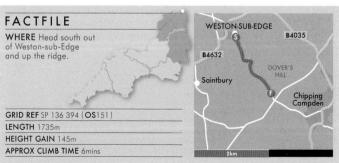

**WHERE** Head south out of Weston-sub-Edge and up the ridge.

WESTON-SUB-EDGE
B4035
B4632
DOVER'S HILL
Saintbury
Chipping Campden
2km

**GRID REF** SP 136 394 (OS151)

**LENGTH** 1735m

**HEIGHT GAIN** 145m

**APPROX CLIMB TIME** 6mins

# SAINTBURY

## SAINTBURY, GLOUCESTERSHIRE

Together with its partner-in-pain Dover's Hill, which lies just to the north, Saintbury is a classic course that's been used for two National Championships, in 1951 and 1960. It's also raced each year as one half of the Warwickshire Road Club two-stage hill climb, with the first leg held on Dover's. Leaving the B4632, the climb rises serenely towards the village, then as the immaculate stone houses with their manicured gardens appear, it ramps up until it reaches its maximum 18% through the left- and right-hand turns. As it exits the village it continues, steep, and you'll now be hurting – but push on as the slope does ease further up. Ahead there's a crossroads, at which point the gradient is a comfortable 5%. Pass through the junction and keep riding. There are a few more stiff ramps still to contend with, maybe peaking at 10% on the way to the golf club; once past, it relents to the summit at the next junction.

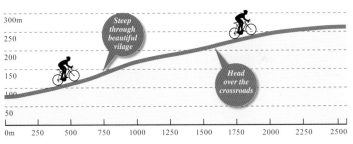

Steep through beautiful village

Head over the crossroads

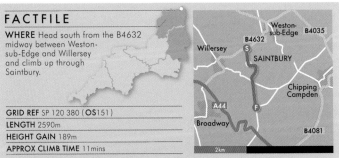

## FACTFILE

**WHERE** Head south from the B4632 midway between Weston-sub-Edge and Willersey and climb up through Saintbury.

**GRID REF** SP 120 380 (OS151)
**LENGTH** 2590m
**HEIGHT GAIN** 189m
**APPROX CLIMB TIME** 11mins

RATING 6/10

# SALTER'S LANE

## WINCHCOMBE, GLOUCESTERSHIRE

There are two ways up to the peak of the ridge that stands to the east of Winchcombe, and of those Salter's Lane is my favourite. The other route, rising directly out of town, is a tough climb but has none of the beauty and open space that you'll find on this ascent. Leaving the base in the tiny village of Hailes, the initial climbing is under tree cover and moderately demanding, up to the first of two cattle grids. Once over this obstacle, the left of the road is for a while lined with a neat hedgerow, before it ends and you begin to pass through open grassland. Surrounded by grazing sheep, the slope is a reasonably heavy 10-11%, so is challenging rather than punishing. The neat and narrow tarmac path weaves across the beautiful land to a second cattle grid, which requires a little more effort to cross. Once over, there's a nasty little steep ramp before the gentle final stretch to the T-junction at the end.

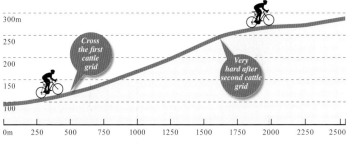

## FACTFILE

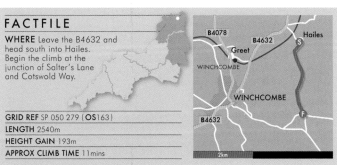

**WHERE** Leave the B4632 and head south into Hailes. Begin the climb at the junction of Salter's Lane and Cotswold Way.

**GRID REF** SP 050 279 (**OS**163)

**LENGTH** 2540m

**HEIGHT GAIN** 193m

**APPROX CLIMB TIME** 11mins

# BUSHCOMBE LANE

## WOODMANCOTE, GLOUCESTERSHIRE

You're spoilt for choice when it comes to climbing Cleeve Hill. The three vicious ascents leaving Woodmancote all offer a fantastic challenge, but it's Bushcombe Lane that stands apart. From the junction with Station Road, exit the village past the first 25% sign, then the road bends left at a second 25% warning – as if you need reminding, this is going to get serious. Once the gradient kicks in it just gets steeper and steeper, 20% past the last of the houses, then the fun really starts. Banking right, the surface breaks up and 20% soon turns into 25%. This is one of the toughest bits of road anywhere in the UK and, through the next left-hand bend, it touches 30% at the apex. Heave yourself round this evil corner and you're through the worst of it. There is still some way to go, but you can click through the gears before finishing just after a gaping cattle grid adjacent to a small car park.

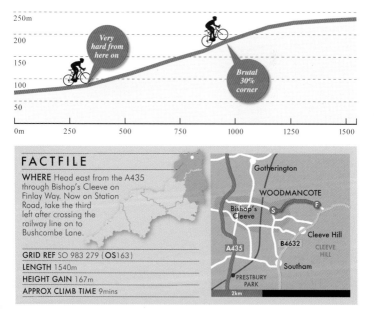

# FACTFILE

**WHERE** Head east from the A435 through Bishop's Cleeve on Finlay Way. Now on Station Road, take the third left after crossing the railway line on to Bushcombe Lane.

**GRID REF** SO 983 279 (**OS**163)

**LENGTH** 1540m

**HEIGHT GAIN** 167m

**APPROX CLIMB TIME** 9mins

# BIRDLIP HILL

Once you've negotiated your way from Cirencester Road, turning right on to Ermin Way, the lower slopes of this climb are comfortable. Passing through Little Witcombe, all is calm until you leave the village and the road turns left into the woods. As the gradient gradually increases you break free of the tree cover then embark on a long 10% straight with fantastic views over your right shoulder. Kinking slightly left, this section of the climb is a real strength-sapper and you must keep on top of your gear because there's plenty more to come. Before the road bends right, take one last look at the view because after that, what would be an even better vista is obscured by lines of tall trees. Continuing hard in their shade on the almost uniform 10% slope, grind your way upwards to the left-hand bend. There the gradient reaches 15%: a cruel ramp to make you work for the summit in the centre of Birdlip.

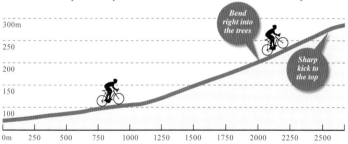

## FACTFILE

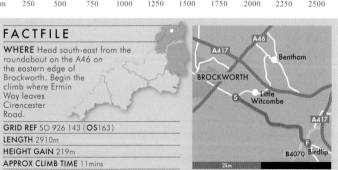

**WHERE** Head south-east from the roundabout on the A46 on the eastern edge of Brockworth. Begin the climb where Ermin Way leaves Cirencester Road.

**GRID REF** SO 926 143 (**OS**163)

**LENGTH** 2910m

**HEIGHT GAIN** 219m

**APPROX CLIMB TIME** 11mins

RATING
5/10

# HARESFIELD BEACON

## HARESFIELD, GLOUCESTERSHIRE

This climb starts in the pleasant surroundings of Haresfield but soon turns wicked on a 20%-gradient stretch. Ease your way out of the village up Beacon Lane to the first test: a collection of smooth, winding bends framed by high hedgerows. These early twists and turns aren't particularly fierce, but will more than likely have you leaving your saddle. Exiting the final bend you ride up to a group of farmhouses, where you're allowed to catch your breath slightly. Make the most of this, because here comes the steep bit: an unforgiving ramp up a rough surface under the cover of trees. This 20% torment ends at a pronounced lump in the tarmac and, as the trees retreat, you can now sit back down to ride the more relaxed slope up to the next brow. This, alas, isn't the summit, but what follows is even more forgiving, and you finally peak adjacent to two large concrete blocks in a field entrance on your left.

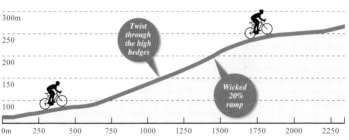

Twist through the high hedges

Wicked 20% ramp

## FACTFILE

**WHERE** Travel south out of Gloucester on the B4008 then turn left on to Haresfield Lane. Cross the M5, pass over the railway bridge, and turn right in front of the school to climb.

**GRID REF** SO 830 086 (OS162)

**LENGTH** 2350m

**HEIGHT GAIN** 200m

**APPROX CLIMB TIME** 12mins

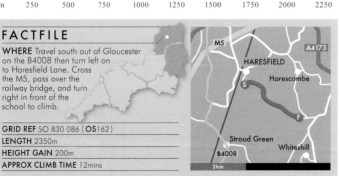

# FROCESTER HILL

A beautiful sweeping ascent with stunning views all the way up, never too steep but always a test – a wonderful climb. Start the ascent from the crossroads at the centre of Frocester and roll out on the moderate, well-surfaced road. Once past the village sign, you're now on the hill, although it's not steep yet; up above, the pristine grassy banks appear shaven, topped with a head of woodland hair. Passing a 10% sign, the road kinks right. The surface, now rougher, eases a bit then rises again, taking you through a well-marked left-hander into a long straight. The gradient is all but uniform – steep, but not unpleasant. You pass through a large S-bend, kinking first right then left, which takes the road via a giant arc into the shelter of the trees at the top. The surface becomes bumpier still, then the road eventually deviates from its constant gradient and eases before finishing abruptly at the junction with the B4066.

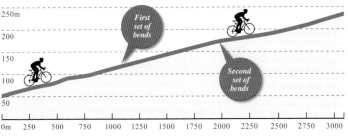

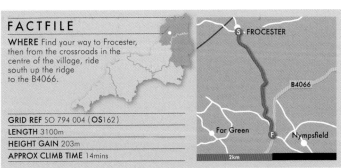

## FACTFILE

**WHERE** Find your way to Frocester, then from the crossroads in the centre of the village, ride south up the ridge to the B4066.

**GRID REF** SO 794 004 (OS162)

**LENGTH** 3100m

**HEIGHT GAIN** 203m

**APPROX CLIMB TIME** 14mins

# SYMONDS YAT

## SYMONDS YAT, GLOUCESTERSHIRE

Just inside the English border on the edge of the Forest of Dean lies Symonds Yat Rock, sitting on a thumb-shaped piece of land surrounded by the River Wye. The wonderful climb to the top of this mound starts on the flat plain at the gates to Huntsham Court Farm, underneath an artistic metal stag's head sitting on a gatepost. It's mild to begin with up to the 'Welcome to Symonds Yat East' sign, then as you climb up through the trees it soon gets hard, approaching 17% in places. You break out of the trees into a brief clearing where the slope eases slightly before you're sent back under more trees and more of the same difficult gradient. Just past the small village with its beautiful stone houses you hit the hardest slopes. It's a proper, tough 20% slog up to the finish. Keep focused on the wooden footbridge that crosses high above the road just shy of the brow – head under that and it's over.

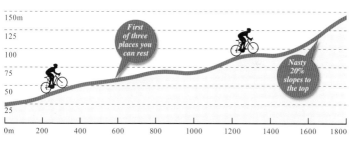

First of three places you can rest

Nasty 20% slopes to the top

## FACTFILE

**WHERE** Leave the B4229 south of Goodrich and head south on the minor road across the River Wye. Pass a few houses and start at the gatepost on your left.

**GRID REF** SO 563 159 (OS162)

**LENGTH** 1800m

**HEIGHT GAIN** 116m

**APPROX CLIMB TIME** 8mins

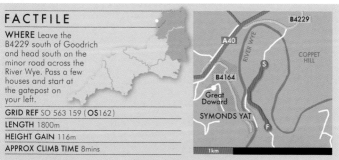

# BEAR HILL

The instant I reached the top of Bear Hill I knew I had to file it under the heading 'The perfect climb' – it's an absolutely stunning little road. The sign at the bottom says 18%, so straight away I knew there was going to be a trial ahead, but what I didn't expect was the beauty, the immaculate surface, the bends… it has it all. First of all you twist slightly left then sharp right – not quite a hairpin – and this is where the slope hits its 18% maximum, but not for long. Still stiff, you rise to the next bend, this time left; from there, you exit the woods on the silky smooth tarmac. Now, bending further right, the road arrives at the base of towering banks – a grassy amphitheatre which places you centre-stage, at its base. The gradient is sublime, the surface perfect. Ahead you'll see the large black bear painted on the pub at the summit: keep your eyes on this, revel in your surroundings and give it everything to the junction at the top.

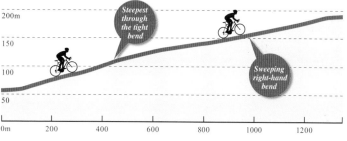

## FACTFILE

**WHERE** Just to the south of Stroud head due east from the A46 at the village of North Woodchester.

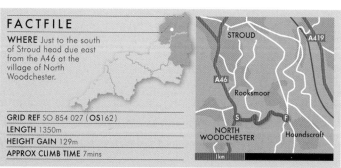

**GRID REF** SO 854 027 (OS162)

**LENGTH** 1350m

**HEIGHT GAIN** 129m

**APPROX CLIMB TIME** 7mins

RATING
6/10

# OAKRIDGE LYNCH

## STROUD, GLOUCESTERSHIRE

Once again I found myself having to make an impossible choice between a number of vicious little climbs out of a particular valley, but I hope you'll agree that the one I picked here is a beauty. From the junction on the bend at its base, the narrow road rises steeply straight away, bending slightly left past a small waterfall. You'll have plenty of momentum in the legs, so no time to stop and admire the cascade before you reach a right-hand corner. The relatively manageable slope continues through the base of the banks; up ahead you'll see the sign for the village and feel some relief. Could this be the top? Of course it isn't, there's lots more hard work to come. The road heads straight up alongside a high stone wall leading you to the centre of the village, but you're still not at the top. A cruel finish awaits as the slope briefly kicks up close to 20%. Head straight on past the roads leading left and right, fighting all the way to the T-junction at the top.

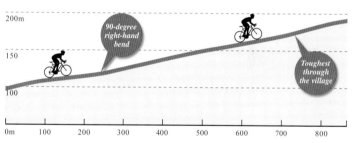

## FACTFILE

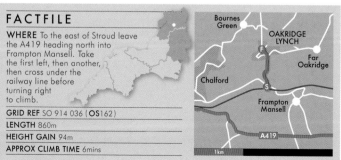

**WHERE** To the east of Stroud leave the A419 heading north into Frampton Mansell. Take the first left, then another, then cross under the railway line before turning right to climb.

**GRID REF** SO 914 036 (OS162)

**LENGTH** 860m

**HEIGHT GAIN** 94m

**APPROX CLIMB TIME** 6mins

RATING

8/10

# OWLPEN HILL

## OWLPEN, GLOUCESTERSHIRE

It's a bit of a convoluted and almost certainly muddy route along the tiny lane out of Uley to find the base of this killer, but trust me, it's worth it. It rolls up and down with a few sharp ramps on the way, but save your effort until you cross the stream and bend south into the woods. The gradient sign at the base has been somewhat suspiciously modified to read 1-in-4 – the road then bends left between a couple of houses. As the slope increases slightly you approach another house then curve right into a canyon of high banks precariously topped with tall trees. The climb is a challenge here but ahead there's a brow and the promise of relief. There isn't any though – it's merely a slight easing before the road, smothered in debris, climbs even steeper. This marks the end of the toil: the road is almost level for a couple of hundred metres before rising gradually past the farm to the finish at the junction.

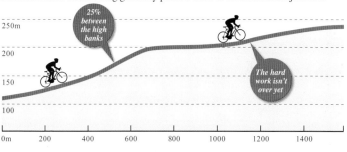

250m

25% between the high banks

200

150

The hard work isn't over yet

100

0m    200    400    600    800    1000    1200    1400

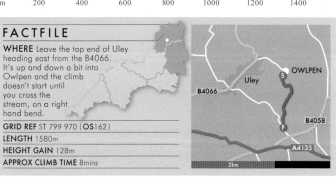

## FACTFILE

**WHERE** Leave the top end of Uley heading east from the B4066. It's up and down a bit into Owlpen and the climb doesn't start until you cross the stream, on a right hand bend.

**GRID REF** ST 799 970 (OS162)

**LENGTH** 1580m

**HEIGHT GAIN** 128m

**APPROX CLIMB TIME** 8mins

# THE BROADWAY

## DURSLEY, GLOUCESTERSHIRE

This vicious little road takes you out of Dursley, up through Cockshoot Wood and on to the plateau of open parkland at the top, in pretty much a straight line. Leaving the roundabout, build up some speed, take the right-hand bend then rise gently past the car park on your left. Up ahead you'll see the 20% sign: the instant you pass it, this is what you'll feel under your wheels. The severity of this initial 50-metre ramp will have you furiously clicking through the gears, then when you reach the corner it's steeper still. Try and ride wide to lessen its impact but take care if you do. Once this obstacle has been negotiated, the slope thankfully begins to subside, although it's never easy. While passing a few houses and into the woods, your screaming legs may just be able to get some strength back for the push to the top. To finish, the harsh gradient returns, not quite as brutal as earlier but enough to make you long for the end.

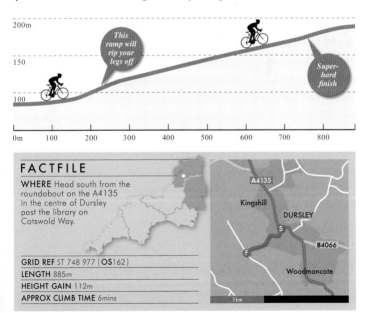

This ramp will rip your legs off

Super-hard finish

## FACTFILE

**WHERE** Head south from the roundabout on the A4135 in the centre of Dursley past the library on Cotswold Way.

Kingshill

DURSLEY

B4066

Woodmancote

**GRID REF** ST 748 977 (**OS**162)

**LENGTH** 885m

**HEIGHT GAIN** 112m

**APPROX CLIMB TIME** 6mins

# HACKPEN HILL

## BROAD HINTON, WILTSHIRE

I've climbed many hillsides adorned with white chalk horses, but none offer as good a view of their primitive art as this climb. As you tick off the opening kilometre it's not only the spindly white steed that's clearly visible but also the distinct path of the road making its way left then right up the grassy ridge. From afar it's a daunting prospect, one that doesn't diminish as you approach the first left-hand corner. The climb rises abruptly here, touching 20% at its apex before easing back on the way to the second bend. The horse is now behind you, to your left are fantastic views out over Wiltshire, and ahead this wonderful climb enters the second bend. The sharp spike in the slope from the next corner will still be in your legs as you sweep round to line yourself up for the big push to the summit, which comes just after the final kink in the road on top of Marlborough Downs.

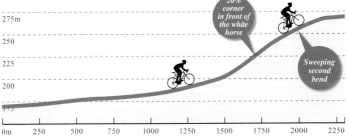

20% corner in front of the white horse

Sweeping second bend

275m
250
225
200
175

0m    250    500    750    1000    1250    1500    1750    2000    2250

## FACTFILE

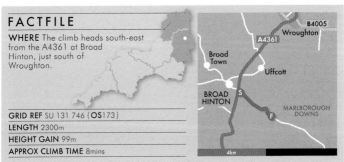

**WHERE** The climb heads south-east from the A4361 at Broad Hinton, just south of Wroughton.

**GRID REF** SU 131 746 (OS173)

**LENGTH** 2300m

**HEIGHT GAIN** 99m

**APPROX CLIMB TIME** 8mins

B4005
Wroughton
A4361
Broad Town
Uffcott
BROAD HINTON
MARLBOROUGH DOWNS
S
F
4km

# MILTON HILL

## MILTON LILBOURNE, WILTSHIRE

I found this climb on the map, double checked it on various websites, studied its statistics and was very excited about taking it on in the flesh. Upon arrival though I nearly didn't make it to the top, as rolling out of Milton, the narrow paved road soon turned to a mess of gravel and mud. I was trying to post a fast time so didn't want to stop, but was it worth it? My head was telling me to turn round – how could I direct people up here? But my heart said just keep going a little further, and I'm so glad I did. Soon enough the gravel finished and although there were a few more patches of rough I was now on a silky-smooth, deathly quiet road winding upwards beneath beautiful grassy banks – but it was hard work. Bending right, the slope kicks up close to 20% in one place, but the struggle in the blissful silence of this hidden gem, finishing high above the plains of Wiltshire, always feels worthwhile.

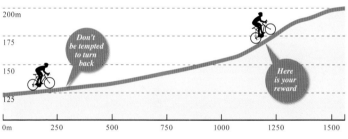

## FACTFILE

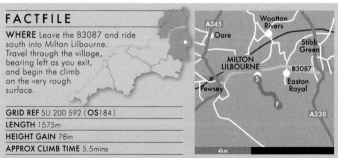

**WHERE** Leave the B3087 and ride south into Milton Lilbourne. Travel through the village, bearing left as you exit, and begin the climb on the very rough surface.

**GRID REF** SU 200 592 (**OS**184)

**LENGTH** 1575m

**HEIGHT GAIN** 78m

**APPROX CLIMB TIME** 5.5mins

# BOWDEN HILL

## BOWDEN HILL, WILTSHIRE

To start this climb, ride past the large National Trust car park at Lacock Abbey, cross the River Avon, and rise sedately into the village of Bowden Hill, which lies nestled among the trees on the hillside. Once past the large expanse of grass to the left, the previously mild gradient bends slowly left around a solitary horse chestnut tree and becomes a bit more of a test. Between the exquisite thatched cottages on either side, the slope is never hideously steep, although does require a substantial effort. Sweeping right, and losing none of its sting, the road lines out to leave the village behind on its way to St Anne's Church. There's a brow here and although it isn't the summit, it marks a distinct change in the energy required. The final 500 metres are comparatively gentle, allowing you to engage a larger gear for the sprint to the summit.

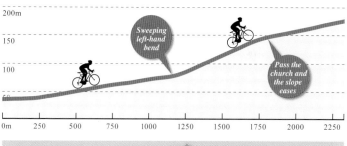

Sweeping left-hand bend

Pass the church and the slope eases

200m
150
100

0m    250    500    750    1000    1250    1500    1750    2000    2250

## FACTFILE

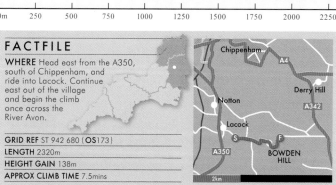

**WHERE** Head east from the A350, south of Chippenham, and ride into Lacock. Continue east out of the village and begin the climb once across the River Avon.

Chippenham
A4
Derry Hill
A342
Notton
Lacock
S
A350
BOWDEN HILL
F
2km

**GRID REF** ST 942 680 (**OS**173)

**LENGTH** 2320m

**HEIGHT GAIN** 138m

**APPROX CLIMB TIME** 7.5mins

# REDHORN HILL

## URCHFONT, WILTSHIRE

Much of the vast Salisbury Plain is forbidden land, military land, the UK's very own Area 51, maybe – so consequently, its glorious open spaces can't be enjoyed on two wheels. There are however a handful of roads that penetrate its edges, roads that lead you up to the lines of barbed wire and overly threatening 'keep out' signs, including this one, which just happens to be an excellent little climb. The approach from the B3098 is arrow-straight and over the first kilometre only rises a handful of metres. As soon as the road bends left at the base of the towering grassy banks, the gradient instantly increases. It's not too tough to begin with, but as you gain altitude over the fields below and climb into the small wood the arduousness increases. Up ahead a right-hand bend comes into view and here is where the stiffest climbing is: push round, bend slightly left then keep riding all the way to the border and its multitude of warnings.

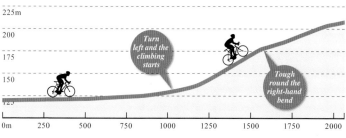

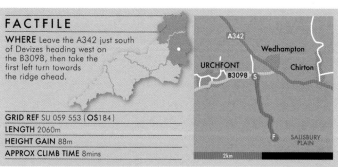

## FACTFILE

**WHERE** Leave the A342 just south of Devizes heading west on the B3098, then take the first left turn towards the ridge ahead.

**GRID REF** SU 059 553 (OS184)

**LENGTH** 2060m

**HEIGHT GAIN** 88m

**APPROX CLIMB TIME** 8mins

RATING
6/10

# WESTBURY HILL

## BRATTON, WILTSHIRE

When approaching this climb from the east, its savage appearance strikes fear into the heart. From some distance away you can see the narrow line of tarmac traversing the bank up to the Westbury White Horse. Leave the main road and ride through the village, then the hedge-lined slope begins to bite. Ahead there's a slight bend and after this the pitch increases by another percentage point. There is very little deviation in direction from here to the summit and not much variation in the gradient either – it's all strenuous. Where you do get a slight easing, make the most of it, spin the legs slightly then be ready to attack when it picks up again. Surrounded by rolling grassland punctuated with the occasional lone tree, you're now ready to tackle the final push to the empty horizon. It's a demanding stretch but keep working, as your efforts will be rewarded with stupendous views once the road breaks right at the eventual summit.

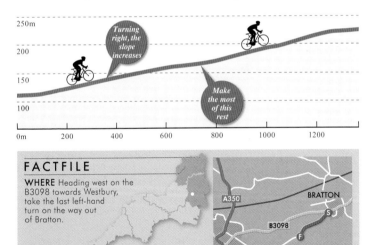

## FACTFILE

**WHERE** Heading west on the B3098 towards Westbury, take the last left-hand turn on the way out of Bratton.

**GRID REF** ST 901 514 (OS184)
**LENGTH** 1375m
**HEIGHT GAIN** 117m
**APPROX CLIMB TIME** 6mins

# PARK HILL

## LONGLEAT, WILTSHIRE

Park Hill is set in the grounds of Longleat, its lowest point sitting adjacent to the magnificent stately home. It feels slightly unnatural to be riding your bike in such a pristine setting but it is permissible to cycle here, and the tarmac is all but perfect. Begin across a cattle grid and look up ahead, as the road appears to have been carefully draped over manicured grassy banks. There's no hedge or wall, no boundary between you and the well-kept grass dotted with neatly placed groups of trees. The road levels past the second cattle grid as it approaches a 90-degree left-hand bend, and then it goes up, steeply. The hardest climbing is at the end – burning legs are burning legs, whether they're on a windswept Welsh mountain or within the confines of what is basically a giant landscaped garden. There's no escaping the effort involved in reaching the top; this is a serious climb in a somewhat bizarre but almost traffic-free environment.

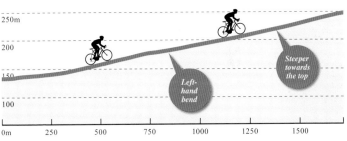

## FACTFILE

**WHERE** Enter Longleat Park and make your way to Longleat House. Start the ascent heading east from the bridge between Half Mile Pond and Ford Pond.

**GRID REF** ST 825 433 (OS183)

**LENGTH** 1740m

**HEIGHT GAIN** 127m

**APPROX CLIMB TIME** 8mins

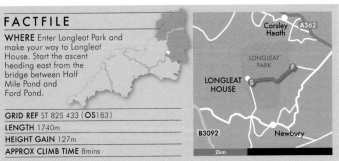

# FOVANT DOWNS

If you're riding west on the A30 into Fovant and glance up, this climb is perfectly presented to provide maximum impact. Looking like a vertical swathe of asphalt cutting through the chalk hillside, it's almost enough to have you bypass the bottom and keep heading west. Of course you won't, though – and fear not, it's not quite as laborious as it first appears. Heading south from the A30, you ease gently upwards towards a right-hand corner where things get tasty. Once round, and past a widening in the road, the slope kicks up to the advertised 15% and higher still, between the tall grassy banks in the shadow of the wall of chalk to your left. Just as this punishing stretch begins to hurt there's a small levelling, but it offers false hope. The next bit is where the real damage is done. Enjoy the brief rest then get out of the saddle for the strenuous push to the top among the trees, where the gradient fizzles away.

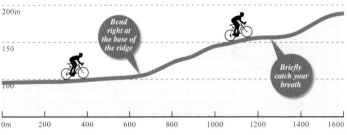

Bend right at the base of the ridge

Briefly catch your breath

## FACTFILE

**WHERE** The climb heads south from the A30 at the southern most point of the village of Fovant which lies just west of Salisbury.

**GRID REF** SU 004 267 (**OS**184)

**LENGTH** 1600m

**HEIGHT GAIN** 95m

**APPROX CLIMB TIME** 5mins

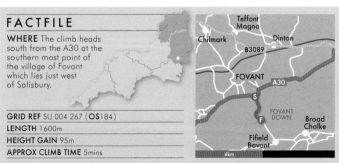

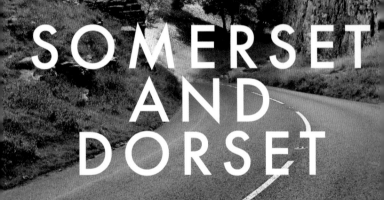

# SOMERSET
# AND
# DORSET

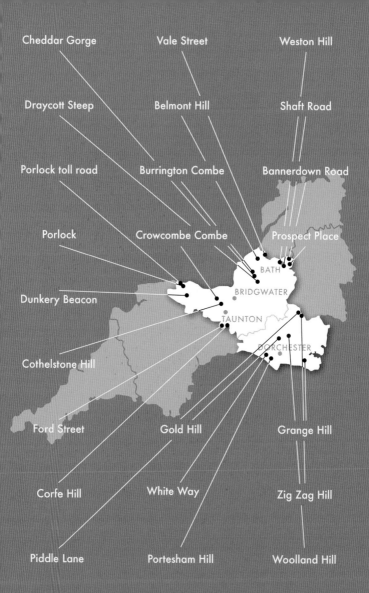

Cheddar Gorge

Vale Street

Weston Hill

Draycott Steep

Belmont Hill

Shaft Road

Porlock toll road

Burrington Combe

Bannerdown Road

Porlock

Crowcombe Combe

Prospect Place

BATH

Dunkery Beacon

BRIDGWATER

TAUNTON

Cothelstone Hill

DORCHESTER

Ford Street

Gold Hill

Grange Hill

Corfe Hill

White Way

Zig Zag Hill

Piddle Lane

Portesham Hill

Woolland Hill

RATING
3/10

# BELMONT HILL

## FAILAND, SOMERSET

There are some days when I wish our roads were built only for cyclists; this is a prime example of a glorious hill that's almost ruined by the presence of traffic. I'm not anti-car, it's just that on the early slopes you can feel quite vulnerable cycling round the tight twists and turns with vehicles racing beside you. So a word of warning: pick a quiet time to ride this climb. Scanning a map, Belmont Hill instantly caught my eye with its series of closely packed bends, and they don't disappoint. To begin with the turns are sharp and the road narrow and steep, then you arrive at a long straight. The road climbs out into the open briefly and you're free from the constraints of those early curves; from here on it feels more free. Head into the second series of sweeping corners, and on a slightly easier slope you reach Failand: don't stop as you enter the village, keep going to the junction with the B3128.

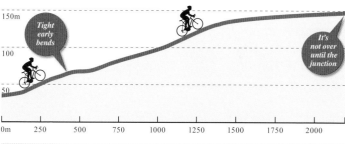

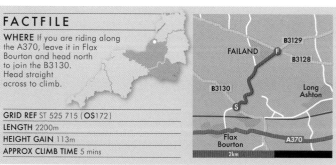

## FACTFILE

**WHERE** If you are riding along the A370, leave it in Flax Bourton and head north to join the B3130. Head straight across to climb.

**GRID REF** ST 525 715 (OS172)

**LENGTH** 2200m

**HEIGHT GAIN** 113m

**APPROX CLIMB TIME** 5 mins

# VALE STREET

Okay, it's no stunning mountain pass, and little more than a novelty, but Vale Street IS the steepest residential road in Europe. Bristol may not be top of your list of cycling destinations but it is a playground of precipitous roads. From afar the houses in this area look as if they are stacked on top of each other, and hidden among them is Vale Street. At first glance it looks impossible, and I'd say on the left-hand side of the road it is – instead of a pavement there's a flight of stairs as it rears up abruptly from Park Street. You're going to need a serious run-up. The thing is, Park Street is all but 20%, so just try to gather what speed you can, turn left, and commit. Your nerves will be racing and you will have to give it everything you've got. Head for the right-hand side of the road and hit it hard. It will take you a matter of seconds to conquer and once through the first 10 metres you're safe – bag it, and then spend a few hours on the surrounding streets.

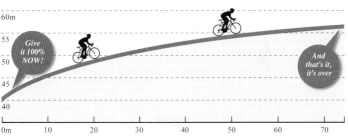

## FACTFILE

**WHERE** Head south out of Bristol on the A4 then turn right on to the A37, Wells Road. Climb the hill then turn left on to School Road, next left down Park Street and the next right is Vale Street.

**GRID REF** ST 603 714 (**OS** 172)

**LENGTH** 74m

**HEIGHT GAIN** 17m

**APPROX CLIMB TIME** 30secs

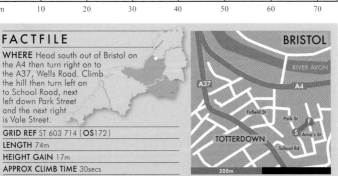

# WESTON HILL

## BATH, SOMERSET

Lansdown Lane leaves Weston in the north-west corner of Bath and heads up the ridge overlooking the city below. Bath is packed full of steep roads, much like its neighbour Bristol, which is great if you like climbing but must be tough on those residents who'd rather have an easier commute to work. With hardly a stretch of flat, you don't have to look far for a decent challenge, but to escape the city, Weston Hill is the route to take. Begin from the roundabout at the head of Weston High Street and pick your way along the rough surface through houses. Soon enough you will have left the urban surroundings behind as you progress up the ridge. The wide road, smoother now on its upper slopes, meanders as it delivers you to its 20% section. Short and sweet, the road banks left, ramps up then kinks right, levelling out 100 metres before the junction with Lansdown Road.

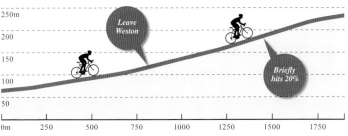

Leave Weston

Briefly hits 20%

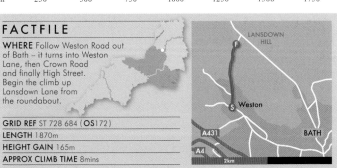

## FACTFILE

**WHERE** Follow Weston Road out of Bath – it turns into Weston Lane, then Crown Road and finally High Street. Begin the climb up Lansdown Lane from the roundabout.

**GRID REF** ST 728 684 (OS172)

**LENGTH** 1870m

**HEIGHT GAIN** 165m

**APPROX CLIMB TIME** 8mins

# BANNERDOWN ROAD

## BATHEASTON, SOMERSET

If you take a look on social media you'll see that Bannerdown Road is a very popular climb for riders in the Bath area. Initially I thought I'd include Steway Lane, which tackles the same ridge just a bit further north, but I was swayed by this climb's popularity so chose to include it instead. There's a reason it's ridden so often: it provides an excellent climbing challenge on a smooth, wide road with a couple of testing spikes in gradient. Start by leaving the roundabout at the base and slowly work your way out of Batheaston. The slope is stiff early on as it sweeps left before crossing a roundabout, but it then eases as it rises alongside a long stone wall. The wall is almost a constant companion as you climb and only ends as you approach the gentle higher slopes, which offer great views out to the right before they peter out to a level.

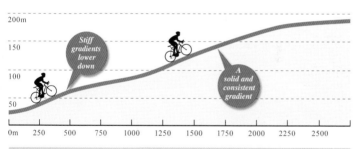

## FACTFILE

**WHERE** From London Road in the centre of Batheaston head north-east on Bannerdown Road from the roundabout.

**GRID REF** ST 795 694 (OS172)

**LENGTH** 2740m

**HEIGHT GAIN** 162m

**APPROX CLIMB TIME** 9mins

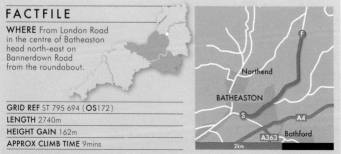

# PROSPECT PLACE

## BATHFORD, SOMERSET

This climb's very short, but trust me, you will not want it to go any further! I rode it on a warm September afternoon; there hadn't been any rain for hours yet the surface was still soaking wet, and when a 25% road is wet, it means just one thing: wheel spin. You can try and help the rear wheel get some more traction by sitting down, but this is easier said than done on a slope this steep. It ramps up instantly from the junction at the base and gets steeper and steeper up to and round the left-hand bend. Once you've negotiated the corner, things get tricky. The surface is pitted and covered with debris – I don't know what was more of a challenge, tackling the gradient or searching for traction. I stuttered and lurched up the precipitous ramp through the woods, begging for it to subside, which naturally it did. Order returns at the junction with Farleigh Rise.

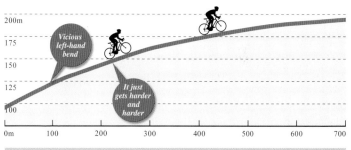

*Vicious left-hand bend*

*It just gets harder and harder*

## FACTFILE

**WHERE** Leave the A4 at the roundabout south of Batheaston and ride into Bathford. Take the first left, ride up through the village then take the last right to climb.

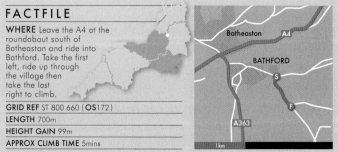

**GRID REF** ST 800 660 (OS172)

**LENGTH** 700m

**HEIGHT GAIN** 99m

**APPROX CLIMB TIME** 5mins

# SHAFT ROAD

## COMBE DOWN, SOMERSET

Originally I'd intended to include Brassknocker Hill to the east, but after riding it I was put off by the amount of traffic. Disappointed, I decided to take a look at Shaft Road on the same ridge – would this be a brilliant climb? What a discovery – it was quiet, filled with twists, flanked by beautiful stone walls, and, best of all, tougher than Brassknocker. Start the climb at the T-junction in the village of Monkton Combe, 20 metres in, and keep right as the road forks. The climbing is steady as you leave the village, then the road rears up after a sharp left-hand bend and heads into a cover of trees. Once through this stretch you approach some houses, levelling as you do. The slope kicks up afterwards; it's not lethal, but still about 17%. It continues, tough, for some distance, snaking between the neat walls up to a 90-degree right-hander, still demanding through the bend then gently regressing to finish outside Bay Tree House.

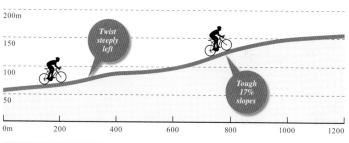

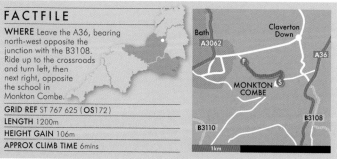

## FACTFILE

**WHERE** Leave the A36, bearing north-west opposite the junction with the B3108. Ride up to the crossroads and turn left, then next right, opposite the school in Monkton Combe.

**GRID REF** ST 767 625 (OS172)

**LENGTH** 1200m

**HEIGHT GAIN** 106m

**APPROX CLIMB TIME** 6mins

# BURRINGTON COMBE

## BURRINGTON, SOMERSET

Always the bridesmaid, never the bride – that's Burrington Combe's lot in life. While its close neighbour, the spectacular Cheddar Gorge, garners all the headlines, it lies rejected, just a couple of miles to the north. Although not as showstopping as its famous cousin, it should not be overlooked; it is a joy to climb. Leaving the T-junction at the base, you are soon rumbling across a cattle grid into the canyon of rock that towers above you. The first kilometre matches any in the country for grandeur and beauty but the dramatic landscape doesn't last for long. Under your wheels the gradient is at worst 10% and there are some nice patches of flat to aid your upward progress. It teases you with a couple of false brows, so it's good to know the climb if you're planning to try and post a fast time, as there's nothing worse than racing for the top only to realise that it isn't the top.

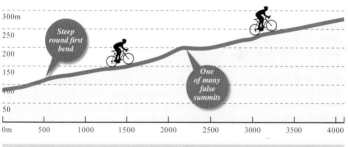

Steep round first bend

One of many false summits

## FACTFILE

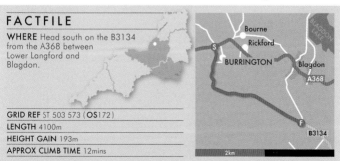

**WHERE** Head south on the B3134 from the A368 between Lower Langford and Blagdon.

| | |
|---|---|
| **GRID REF** ST 503 573 (**OS**172) | |
| **LENGTH** 4100m | |
| **HEIGHT GAIN** 193m | |
| **APPROX CLIMB TIME** 12mins | |

# CHEDDAR GORGE

## CHEDDAR, SOMERSET

Cut deep into the Mendip Hills lies Cheddar Gorge, a natural phenomenon that makes a stunning setting to climb through. Start from a little plateau alongside a pond and then pass some gift shops; the asphalt kicks up steep through large car parks on either side of the road. The surface is excellent and the road is wide and, like Box Hill in Surrey, you will always find cyclists on its slopes as it offers a tough but not overwhelming challenge to riders of all abilities. With the gorge's rock faces towering around you, you'll soon reach the hardest 16% section. A couple of sweeping bends and you're through the worst; as the sides of the gorge diminish, so does the severity of the slope. This climb can flatter the rider like no other – the higher you climb the easier it gets and the faster you move. With each revolution you'll gain momentum; click up through the gears and finish with a flourish as the road flattens on the hilltop.

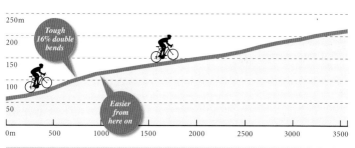

## FACTFILE

**WHERE** Leave the A37, Church Street, and turn onto the B3135, Union Street. This turns into Cliff Street and then The Cliffs, which leads you to the base just past Cox's Cave.

**GRID REF** ST 485 535 (OS172)

**LENGTH** 3540m

**HEIGHT GAIN** 150m

**APPROX CLIMB TIME** 13mins

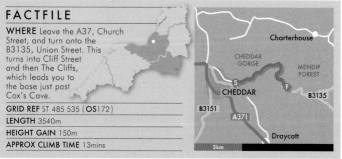

# DRAYCOTT STEEP

## DRAYCOTT, SOMERSET

Rising up the same ridge and gaining a similar amount of altitude as Cheddar Gorge, but at close to half its length, Draycott Steep is a much more daunting prospect than its neighbour. This road doesn't bother twisting and winding its way to the top of the Mendips, it just heads straight up, as the crow flies, and consequently hurts – a lot. Reasonably stiff through the village, it just gets tougher and tougher upon leaving, the gradient increasing ever so slightly with every pedal rev. It creeps up on you like a ninja in the night – you will all of a sudden find you're out of the saddle on the largest sprocket and underneath your wheels is a gruelling 20% slope. Ahead the brow is your saviour – drag yourself over and the second half of the climb is much easier. No walk in the park, as like the first stretch this part ramps up ever so slightly the further it climbs, but thankfully it's nowhere near as steep. Then, you can finally relax.

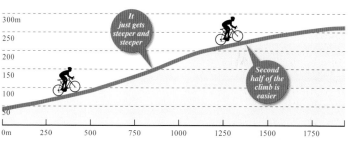

It just gets steeper and steeper

Second half of the climb is easier

## FACTFILE

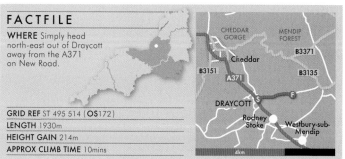

**WHERE** Simply head north-east out of Draycott away from the A371 on New Road.

| | |
|---|---|
| **GRID REF** ST 495 514 (OS172) | |
| **LENGTH** 1930m | |
| **HEIGHT GAIN** 214m | |
| **APPROX CLIMB TIME** 10mins | |

# CROWCOMBE COMBE

## CROWCOMBE, SOMERSET

Running in an almost dead-straight line from the base to the summit of the Quantock Hills lies the tough climb out of Crowcombe. For the perfect hill to race up – one that will really suit the true climbers – look no further. This short, quiet stretch of road has plenty of 25% gradient, ample parking at its base, and natural banks for spectators. It's hard from the very start; leave the village and veer left, through the trees, past the 1-in-4 sign where the road levels slightly adjacent to an escape lane for runaway vehicles. The super-smooth road heads up direct and steep, first at 20%, then for a short while 25%, before easing back to 20% and bending gently to the right. Near the summit comes the hardest section: a left-hand bend ushering in 30 metres of leg-breaking 25%. Eventually it levels as you enter some woods and rumble – stars in your eyes – across a cattle grid to finish.

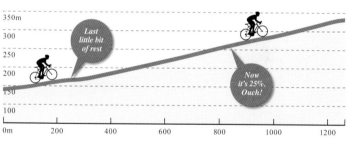

## FACTFILE

**WHERE** Heading north, leave the A358 just past Flaxpool and turn into Crowcombe. Ride to the centre of the village, turn east opposite the car park, and head upwards.

**GRID REF** ST 149 374 (OS181)

**LENGTH** 1270m

**HEIGHT GAIN** 188m

**APPROX CLIMB TIME** 8.5mins

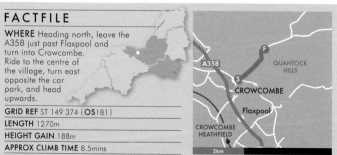

RATING
7/10

# COTHELSTONE HILL

## COTHELSTONE, SOMERSET

Although not quite as onerous as nearby Crowcombe Combe, Cothelstone Hill is nonetheless a brute of a climb. The first kilometre is very steady, rising ever so slightly on the narrow road between high hedgerows. Bending right then left round a smattering of buildings, the slope begins to liven up as it enters the heart of Cothelstone. Passing a grand stone arch on your left, things begins to get interesting on the approach to the 90-degree left-hand bend where – BAM – it's now seriously steep. Creeping up the side of the ridge with wonderful views out to the left, it starts to bend slightly right into a tunnel of trees. The higher you ride the more laborious it is, until, approaching a pronounced right-hand bend, the slope creeps up to its maximum 20%. As you leave the grand vistas behind, the final 500 metres to the summit seem tame when compared to what you have just ridden but still require some effort to complete.

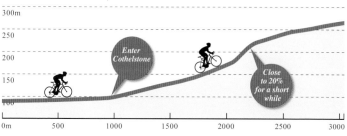

## FACTFILE

**WHERE** Leave the A358 at Bishops Lydeard and head into the village on Station Road. Continue north through the village and begin the climb at the crossroads.

**GRID REF** ST 189 331 (OS193)

**LENGTH** 3030m

**HEIGHT GAIN** 179m

**APPROX CLIMB TIME** 11mins

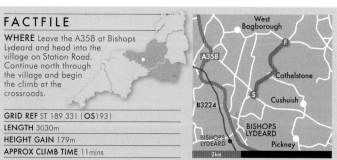

# FORD STREET

## WELLINGTON, SOMERSET

I had to choose one from four climbs I'd highlighted along the northern ridge of the Blackdown Hills. I quickly discounted Combe Hill: too ordinary, not long enough. I almost went for the road out of Angersleigh, which is pretty steep but lacks drama. That left me with Blagdon Hill and Ford Street. Blagdon almost got the nod because of its wonderful hairpin, but Ford Street has the most to offer. Start your ascent from under the M5 and ascend gently into the village where the road all but levels. As it rises away from the small collection of houses, you can see the pitch of the road visibly increase. From here on it's effortful work with prolonged stretches of 8% gradient through the gentle twists and turns in the woods. Once through the curves, the road bends right into an even stiffer stretch up to a devilish left-hand bend that really makes you work for the summit.

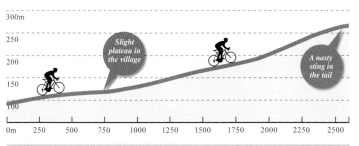

*Slight plateau in the village*

*A nasty sting in the tail*

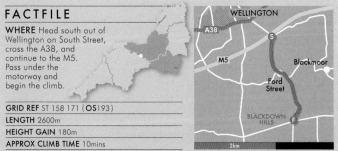

## FACTFILE

**WHERE** Head south out of Wellington on South Street, cross the A38, and continue to the M5. Pass under the motorway and begin the climb.

**GRID REF** ST 158 171 (OS193)

**LENGTH** 2600m

**HEIGHT GAIN** 180m

**APPROX CLIMB TIME** 10mins

# CORFE HILL

The road that turns into Corfe Hill rises just about all the way from the centre of Taunton, but for argument's sake and to avoid a lot of congestion it's easier to say the climb starts in the village of Corfe. It's the most prominent and busiest route up the northern edge of the Blackdown Hills and also the longest, but by no means the hardest. The slope is an almost uniform 6% to 7% from start to finish, only wavering a fraction here and there from its steady but still challenging incline. As you leave the village there's soon the first of two right turns to the shorter and far steeper Old Combe Hill if you fancy a tougher climb; if not, stick to the kinder slopes that you're already on. Work your way upwards through the tree-lined, meandering curves that flow left and right through the woods to reach the summit at the crossroads and the eastern edge of the ridge.

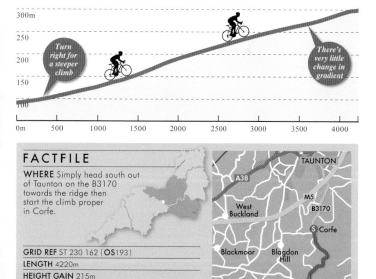

## FACTFILE

**WHERE** Simply head south out of Taunton on the B3170 towards the ridge then start the climb proper in Corfe.

**GRID REF** ST 230 162 (OS193)

**LENGTH** 4220m

**HEIGHT GAIN** 215m

**APPROX CLIMB TIME** 11mins

# DUNKERY BEACON

## PORLOCK, SOMERSET

This corner of Exmoor is hill-climbing heaven, with a plethora of nasty roads to grind up and fly down. It's a job to single out one climb that sets itself apart from all others, but the road heading away from Luccombe up to the Beacon is a beast. Leave the crossroads and head into thick forest. Ramping up straight away at 17% and winding across a steep cattle grid, the road heads upwards under the trees. With the opening stretch over, your legs will already be burning by the time the gradient affords you a brief rest. And then it climbs again – if you thought the first part was a trial, think again. A perfect stretch of unrelenting 17% gradient cuts its way through the gorse, turning left then right, steeper at each turn, before delivering you to the finale. Ahead, the road winds like a streamer dropped from a tall building, kinking left and right, left and right, steep all the way. You'll finish, consumed by fatigue, adjacent to a small stone car park.

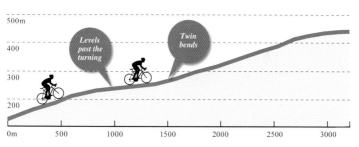

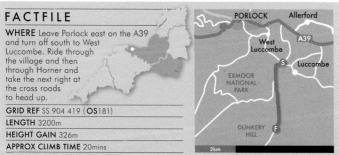

## FACTFILE

**WHERE** Leave Porlock east on the A39 and turn off south to West Luccombe. Ride through the village and then through Horner and take the next right at the cross roads to head up.

**GRID REF** SS 904 419 (OS181)

**LENGTH** 3200m

**HEIGHT GAIN** 326m

**APPROX CLIMB TIME** 20mins

# PORLOCK

As the road climbs out of Porlock, heading west towards Lynmouth, you see the warning sign: gradient 1-in-4. Uphill! This isn't for the faint-hearted. Pass the sign, easing left, and there in front of you, rising like a skyscraper, is the fearsome 1-in-4 right-hand bend. Wrench your bike into the darkness under the trees and grind along more of the same gradient to the next bend, this time a left-hander and steeper, nigh on vertical at its apex, where you are forced to the centre of the road in order to keep momentum. It banks right, now just at 1-in-5, and the air is filled with the stench of burning clutches from vehicles as they struggle past. A false summit marks the end of the back-breaking lower slopes, and now a much more manageable gradient takes you further up the ridge. After another brow in the road there's one final hard stretch to go before you can stop to admire the view of the coast in the distance below.

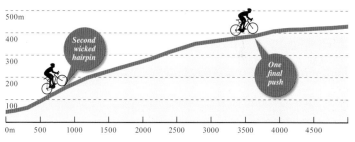

## FACTFILE

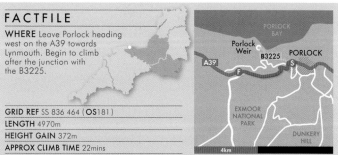

**WHERE** Leave Porlock heading west on the A39 towards Lynmouth. Begin to climb after the junction with the B3225.

**GRID REF** SS 836 464 (OS181)
**LENGTH** 4970m
**HEIGHT GAIN** 372m
**APPROX CLIMB TIME** 22mins

RATING
3/10

# PORLOCK TOLL ROAD

## PORLOCK, SOMERSET

I'd ridden the escape from Porlock up the A39 a number of times, drawn by its fierce 25% gradient, and although I was aware of the toll road I never gave it much thought. I guess I was put off by the word 'toll'. So when I found out there was a race organised on it, and the £1 fee would be waived, I couldn't resist making the journey to check it out. Wow, just wow: what a road. Quiet as a mouse, set on a perfectly pitched slope, winding like an Alpine mountain lane through thick forest, and then delivering you on to the blissful open moors at the top: the Porlock toll road is faultless. The first 4.5 kilometres are played out in the protection of trees, twisting and turning upwards, and there are even two tight hairpins either side of the toll booth. Once out into the open land further up, a prevailing wind may slow your progress as you gaze out over Porlock Bay, but even a hurricane couldn't diminish the enjoyment of this climb.

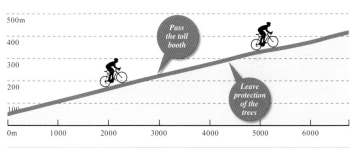

## FACTFILE

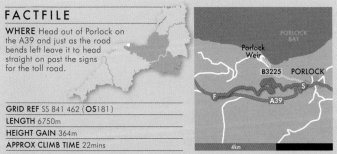

**WHERE** Head out of Porlock on the A39 and just as the road bends left leave it to head straight on past the signs for the toll road.

**GRID REF** SS 841 462 (OS181)

**LENGTH** 6750m

**HEIGHT GAIN** 364m

**APPROX CLIMB TIME** 22mins

# GOLD HILL

## SHAFTESBURY, DORSET

Gold Hill is the centrepiece of the most picture-perfect chocolate-box scene in the whole of Britain. Immortalised by the famous Hovis bread TV ad, the view from the top attracts visitors from every corner of the globe. So if you're going to attempt this climb then beware, for as soon as you begin your ascent you too will become part of the attraction. Your every strained revolution will be scrutinised as your effort becomes entertainment – you dare not fail to reach the top now. Start at the junction with Layton Lane. Following a brief stretch of tarmac the cobbles begin; it is extremely steep and the stones are also greasy and uneven, so try to stay seated to aid traction. To make matters worse, every 10 metres or so you cross a ridge of larger stones that hit like waves. You will be constantly forced to find the better line, as if navigating an uphill maze, to finish in the small sloping plaza in front of the café.

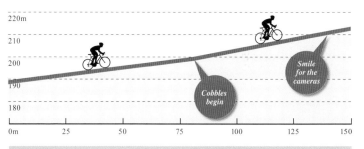

Cobbles begin

Smile for the cameras

## FACTFILE

**WHERE** The climb begins where Layton Lane (from the east) and St James Street (from the west) meet. Turn north on to Gold Hill and head up.

| | |
|---|---|
| **GRID REF** ST 862 229 (OS183) | |
| **LENGTH** 150m | |
| **HEIGHT GAIN** 24m | |
| **APPROX CLIMB TIME** 2mins | |

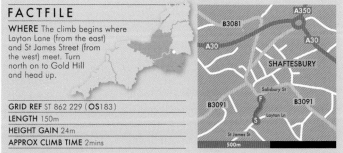

# ZIG ZAG HILL

## SHAFTESBURY, DORSET

Just south of Shaftesbury sit the sweeping, tangled bends of Zig Zag Hill. This mini-mountainesque ascent is perfect for riders wanting to hone their uphill cornering technique before heading off to the Alps or the Pyrenees. The climb begins where the tarmac changes colour; the surface is really rugged and there are also deep-set iron grilles to avoid. The first of the three hairpins is a tight right-hander, the next a left – after this the road bends right, tight left, right and into the third hairpin. Ride smoothly into the bends, and as the road levels slightly don't change gear – spin the small one, offering the legs a short rest, then build a fraction more momentum before you exit and begin to push again. The slopes are steepest at the bottom, but not outrageous at 10%. Round a final sweeping left-hand bend and you exit the trees to ride the smooth upper part into Wiltshire. Crest the brow just past a large car park on your right.

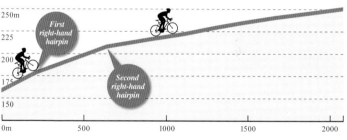

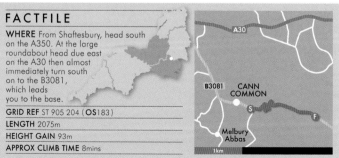

## FACTFILE

**WHERE** From Shaftesbury, head south on the A350. At the large roundabout head due east on the A30 then almost immediately turn south on to the B3081, which leads you to the base.

**GRID REF** ST 905 204 (**OS**183)

**LENGTH** 2075m

**HEIGHT GAIN** 93m

**APPROX CLIMB TIME** 8mins

# WOOLLAND HILL

## WOOLLAND, DORSET

There are two great climbs to the top of this mound: Bulbarrow Hill, climbing through Stoke Wake, and this one, Woolland Hill. Once you've found the base you begin to rise into the village and climb gently through and out the other side. As the road bends right the slope increases in severity for a short while before levelling as it runs along the top edge of Woolland and past the church. Next it turns 90 degrees left, and here is probably the hardest part of the climb, under the trees between the high hedgerows. Once round the next bend the views open up to your right, the slope eases, and on the hilltop ahead you'll see the radio mast – it's instantly apparent you're still far from the top. You're rewarded with spectacular views for the rest of the ride, so make sure you keep glancing right while you home in on the tough finale to the junction with Bulbarrow Hill.

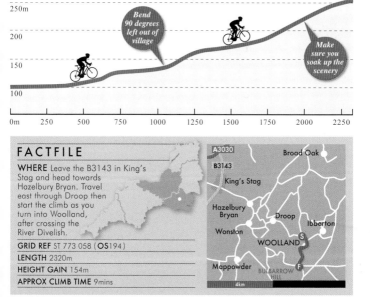

Bend 90 degrees left out of village

Make sure you soak up the scenery

## FACTFILE

**WHERE** Leave the B3143 in King's Stag and head towards Hazelbury Bryan. Travel east through Droop then start the climb as you turn into Woolland, after crossing the River Divelish.

**GRID REF** ST 773 058 (OS194)

**LENGTH** 2320m

**HEIGHT GAIN** 154m

**APPROX CLIMB TIME** 9mins

# PIDDLE LANE

## CERNE ABBAS, DORSET

Heading east from Cerne Abbas, Piddle Lane features a difficult start. As you take a narrow right turn you're thrust into a stretch of rough and tough climbing. It's short, however, so don't be afraid to give it some stick, because you'll be rewarded with a decent rest afterwards where you can click down a couple of sprockets. Next follows another ramp, shorter than the first, which is again followed by more simple climbing before the long trudge to the finish begins. Ahead you see the road visibly rise steeper into the woods and then bend out of view. The slope soon reaches its maximum 17% and is stiff all the way to the corner and round it. And it's not over – this last bit is harder still to the brow, which seems to move away the closer you get, prolonging the agony and postponing the relief of cresting the summit, which lies just past the farm next to the water treatment plant.

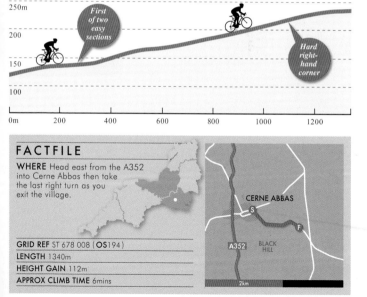

## FACTFILE

**WHERE** Head east from the A352 into Cerne Abbas then take the last right turn as you exit the village.

| | |
|---|---|
| **GRID REF** ST 678 008 (OS194) | |
| **LENGTH** 1340m | |
| **HEIGHT GAIN** 112m | |
| **APPROX CLIMB TIME** 6mins | |

RATING
6/10

# WHITE WAY

## LITTON CHENEY, DORSET

Amid the collection of little hills up the ridge to the A35, it's White Way that can claim to be the most strenuous, and it's a significant test. It's a climb of two distinct halves: the wicked gradients on the lower slopes under the canopy of trees, where the real damage will be done, and the more gentle, yet seemingly no less arduous and slightly longer, stretch to the summit. Begin the climb by heading north from Litton Cheney, passing the tree that bisects the road at the base and the 1-in-4 sign. Immediately it's hard. I'm not sure it quite reaches the advertised gradient, but it's certainly a struggle up to a slight easing off, then it's labour-intensive once more all the way until you exit the trees. Here the gradient backs off, but your legs will be sore. You may be able to click up a sprocket, or simply sit down for a while and begin a different sort of effort – instead of pushing the gear, now you can spin it all the way to the finish.

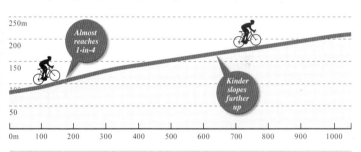

Almost reaches 1-in-4

Kinder slopes further up

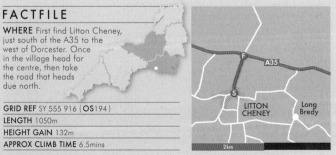

## FACTFILE

**WHERE** First find Litton Cheney, just south of the A35 to the west of Dorcester. Once in the village head for the centre, then take the road that heads due north.

**GRID REF** SY 555 916 (OS194)

**LENGTH** 1050m

**HEIGHT GAIN** 132m

**APPROX CLIMB TIME** 6.5mins

# PORTESHAM HILL

## PORTESHAM, DORSET

It's somewhat perverse to be looking for pain and suffering in a part of the country that is so quaint and beautiful, but who wants quaint and beautiful – bring on the pain! Start the climb from the B3157 and rise steadily through the village to the junction with Back Street. Here's where the climb becomes Portesham Hill, and the action begins as the road widens; the ridge approaches and the sign says 17%. It's slightly steeper at the bottom as it starts to bend left, and you'll be forced out of the saddle. The further left it bends the harder it becomes, until its course changes right and its complexion changes. The high grassy banks that shadowed you until now have all but faded away and ahead you'll see the brow. The end of the steep climbing is definitive and instant, although it's not quite the summit as there is a small amount of altitude still to be gained to the junction ahead.

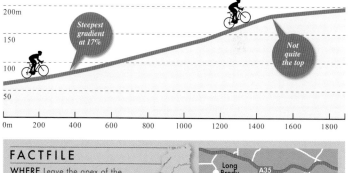

Steepest gradient at 17%

Not quite the top

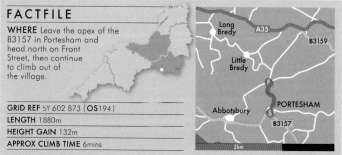

## FACTFILE

**WHERE** Leave the apex of the B3157 in Portesham and head north on Front Street, then continue to climb out of the village.

**GRID REF** SY 602 873 (OS194)

**LENGTH** 1880m

**HEIGHT GAIN** 132m

**APPROX CLIMB TIME** 6mins

# GRANGE HILL

## WAREHAM, DORSET

You could argue that this climb starts from the junction of the A351, but it's not until you pass under a railway line that you begin to feel the gradient bite. The first section of the ascent is like a giant set of stairs with three ramps followed by three plateaus – not severe, but plenty tough enough to warm the legs up. After these tests you enter the village of Creech and the climb levels significantly. The road is lined either side by old, neat metal fences; up ahead you see a familiar red triangle, and inside it is the warning of 20% slopes ahead. The killer finish awaits. Bending right at the base of the ridge the gradient kicks up straight away and it's not long before you're toiling out of the saddle, weaving the bike left and right to fight gravity. Keep pushing up on the seemingly ever-steepening slope to the abrupt corner at the junction on the apex of the ridge, from where there are wonderful views in all directions.

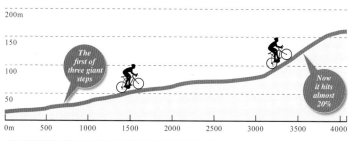

The first of three giant steps

Now it hits almost 20%

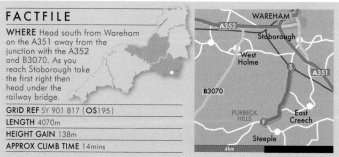

## FACTFILE

**WHERE** Head south from Wareham on the A351 away from the junction with the A352 and B3070. As you reach Stoborough take the first right then head under the railway bridge.

**GRID REF** SY 901 817 (OS195)

**LENGTH** 4070m

**HEIGHT GAIN** 138m

**APPROX CLIMB TIME** 14mins

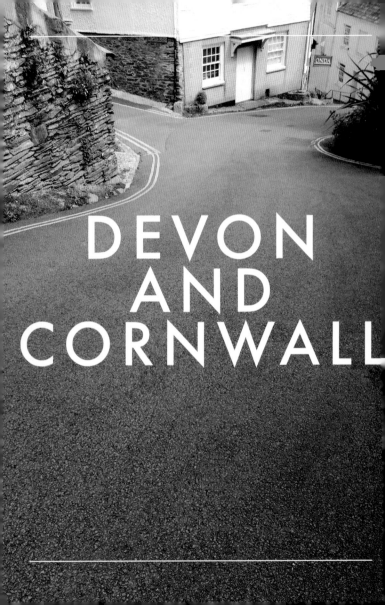

# DEVON
# AND
# CORNWALL

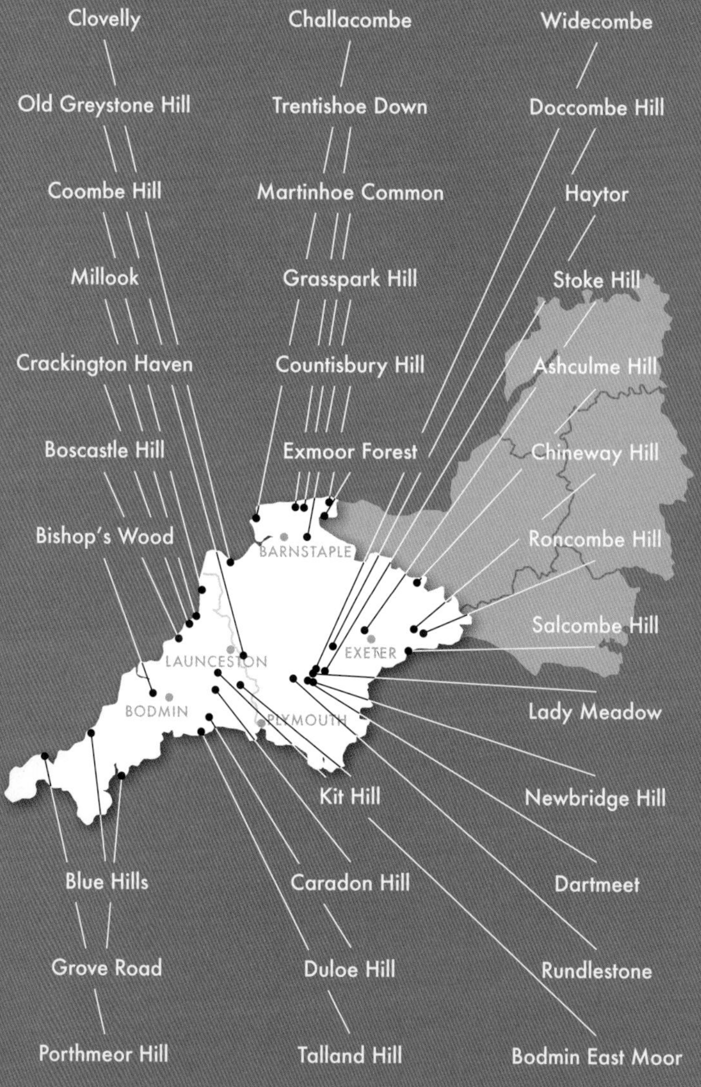

Clovelly

Challacombe

Widecombe

Old Greystone Hill

Trentishoe Down

Doccombe Hill

Coombe Hill

Martinhoe Common

Haytor

Millook

Grasspark Hill

Stoke Hill

Crackington Haven

Countisbury Hill

Ashculme Hill

Boscastle Hill

Exmoor Forest

Chineway Hill

Bishop's Wood

Roncombe Hill

BARNSTAPLE

Salcombe Hill

EXETER

LAUNCESTON

BODMIN

Lady Meadow

PLYMOUTH

Kit Hill

Newbridge Hill

Blue Hills

Caradon Hill

Dartmeet

Grove Road

Duloe Hill

Rundlestone

Porthmeor Hill

Talland Hill

Bodmin East Moor

# COUNTISBURY HILL

## LYNMOUTH, DEVON

One of three great climbs that leave Lynmouth, Countisbury Hill takes you east offering fantastic views out over the Bristol Channel. Begin the climb immediately as you leave town and it's straight up. The sign says 25% as you head into darkness under the trees, but this seems a bit of an exaggeration, it feels more like 20%. As you exit the trees into daylight overlooking Lynmouth Bay, you're through the toughest stretch and, legs burning, you see your next task ahead of you. The long, steady climb, coarsely surfaced, makes it heavy going, but once your legs have recovered from the abrupt start the even gradient will allow you to find a good rhythm. The route snakes left and right as it follows the coastline, climbing all the time as it approaches Countisbury. Then it levels, dips, and rears up once more – this time up to 16%. Now you have the final long push to the top, situated at the apex of a sweeping left-hand bend.

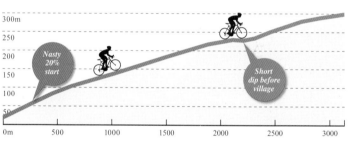

## FACTFILE

**WHERE** Leave the centre of Lynmouth and head east up and out of town on the A39.

**GRID REF** SS 753 494 (OS180)
**LENGTH** 3115m
**HEIGHT GAIN** 284m
**APPROX CLIMB TIME** 15mins

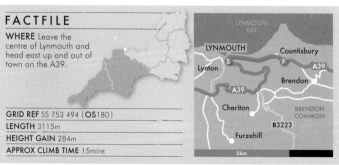

# EXMOOR FOREST

## LYNMOUTH, DEVON

The town of Lynmouth lies at the base of three stiff climbs – the very tough Countisbury Hill, the shorter and steeper Lynton Hill, and finally the long road heading up onto Exmoor. It's this route from sea level to the top of Hoar Tor that provides the most climbing. A tiny kick out of town soon eases into a steady gradient as the road follows the river through the valley. Past a car park, you reach the left turn for the B3223 and cross the bridge onto the harder inclines. You wouldn't expect to reach the top of Exmoor without some serious toil and this middle stretch gives you just that. Keep pushing and you'll reach a couple of hairpin bends – first left, then back on yourself, then right – which deliver you on to the gentler higher slopes. Now above the trees, the well-surfaced but rough-topped road, populated by sheep, grinds on and on, finally petering out just before Blackpitts Gate.

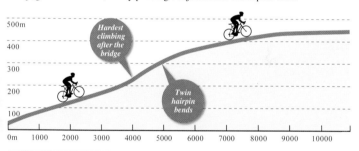

Hardest climbing after the bridge

Twin hairpin bends

## FACTFILE

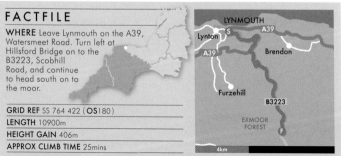

**WHERE** Leave Lynmouth on the A39, Watersmeet Road. Turn left at Hillsford Bridge on to the B3223, Scobhill Road, and continue to head south on to the moor.

| | |
|---|---|
| **GRID REF** SS 764 422 ( **OS**180) | |
| **LENGTH** 10900m | |
| **HEIGHT GAIN** 406m | |
| **APPROX CLIMB TIME** 25mins | |

RATING 7/10

# TRENTISHOE DOWN

## KEMACOTT, DEVON

Roads simply do not come any more beautiful than this: I was utterly gobsmacked when I reached the top. From the gnarled trees and moss-covered walls on the winding lower slopes to the gorse-lined open path that leads to the barren summit and its stunning views out to sea, I must have stopped a dozen times just to soak it all in. Leaving the Hunters Inn, ignore the tempting 25% signs at the bottom of Trentishoe Lane on your left and head due west into the cavern of twisted trees. Weaving upwards, with one pronounced left-hand hairpin, the slope is a continuous challenge, hitting 16% in places. Before long it leaves the woods to reveal spectacular views out over the bay. For a while the gradient relents significantly and you'll see the route passing over the mound ahead; the hardest part of the finale is not the climb but focusing on the road instead of looking out to sea.

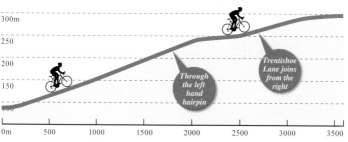

Through the left hand hairpin

Trentishoe Lane joins from the right

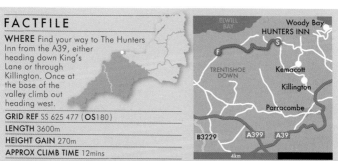

## FACTFILE

**WHERE** Find your way to The Hunters Inn from the A39, either heading down King's Lane or through Killington. Once at the base of the valley climb out heading west.

**GRID REF** SS 625 477 (OS180)

**LENGTH** 3600m

**HEIGHT GAIN** 270m

**APPROX CLIMB TIME** 12mins

# MARTINHOE COMMON

## KEMACOTT, DEVON

Whilst heading to Trentishoe Down I first had to ride down from Martinhoe Common along this road. I hadn't given it much thought prior to arrival but what I was met with was a masterpiece. On a sunny spring afternoon, the lush greenery juxtaposed with the rugged, worn, twisting, and in places brutally steep road was a wonder to behold. Once at the bottom I turned right round and rode back up it. Starting on King's Lane, it's immediately tough past the 25% gradient sign and it never gives in. On and on it rises, harshly through the woods, a sinuous strip of tarmac bisecting beautiful surroundings, and then comes a wicked right-hand hairpin. Once round, there's no let-up until you pass a cottage on your left; then and only then can you take a breather. Now high up the bank, you ride up to and across Cherryford Lane before continuing the strength-sapping drag to the eventual summit.

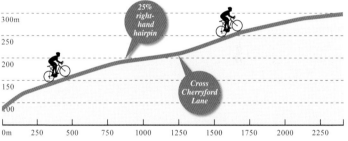

FACTFILE

**WHERE** Find your way to The Hunters Inn by riding east over Trentishoe Down, or heading north from the A39 via Killington. From the inn head east up King's Lane.

**GRID REF** SS 676 475 (OS180)

**LENGTH** 2400m

**HEIGHT GAIN** 230m

**APPROX CLIMB TIME** 11mins

33%

Unsuitable
for heavy
goods vehicles

RATING
7/10

# GRASSPARK HILL

If you want to make the initial part of this climb as comfortable as possible, you must hit it at speed and be ready in a small gear. It caught me by surprise and I ended up having to do a bit of a U-turn to shift the chain off the big ring. So sudden is its impact that it will bring you to a dead halt if you are not prepared. Heading up between the hedgerows, it's at the first left-hand corner where the climb reaches its advertised 33%, maybe only momentarily, but enough to make you wince. And it's not over – as you continue round a right-hand bend, the slope remains drastically steep for a few more metres. Now the gradient gradually abates, until the road reaches the brow at the Charles village sign, where there follows a tiny downhill. At the junction in the village keep right and push on north until you're no longer gaining altitude.

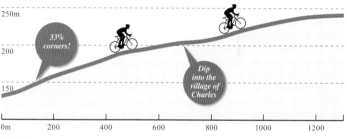

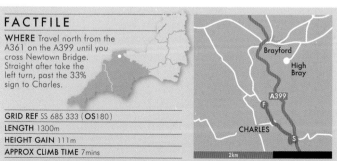

## FACTFILE

**WHERE** Travel north from the A361 on the A399 until you cross Newtown Bridge. Straight after take the left turn, past the 33% sign to Charles.

| | |
|---|---|
| **GRID REF** | SS 685 333 (OS180) |
| **LENGTH** | 1300m |
| **HEIGHT GAIN** | 111m |
| **APPROX CLIMB TIME** | 7mins |

# CHALLACOMBE

## WOOLACOMBE, DEVON

Like so many coastal villages, Woolacombe lies hemmed in next to the sea by the surrounding cliffs, the only access to it being the steep roads that pick their way to the shore. Challacombe Hill is one of the steepest, and it's been used for races for many years. During the summer you'll find it busy with people pushing their hire bikes up to the campsites at the top, having enjoyed an exhilarating ride to the beach that morning. Start the climb just out of town, pass several caravan parks and bend right. It rises up hard immediately and never gives you a rest. The single-track, well-surfaced road creeps away from the bustle of the small town, kinking left slightly around midway. Higher up it hits 25% and the tarmac begins to ripple, resembling wavelets on the shore below. You'll find it very hard going as you are jolted along the final metres that lead to the top.

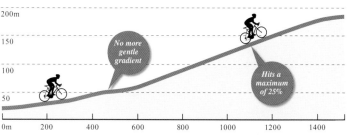

No more gentle gradient

Hits a maximum of 25%

200m

150

100

50

0m    200    400    600    800    1000    1200    1400

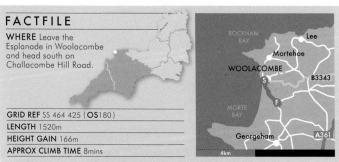

## FACTFILE

**WHERE** Leave the Esplanade in Woolacombe and head south on Challacombe Hill Road.

**GRID REF** SS 464 425 (**OS**180)

**LENGTH** 1520m

**HEIGHT GAIN** 166m

**APPROX CLIMB TIME** 8mins

ROCKHAM BAY
Lee
Mortehoe
WOOLACOMBE
S
B3343
MORTE BAY
F
Georgeham
A361
4km

RATING
8/10

# CLOVELLY

## CLOVELLY, DEVON

It's not possible to ride the cobbled streets of traffic-free Clovelly, but there is a road you can ride – the incredibly precipitous, private-access route that's used by 4x4s to ferry the many visitors to and from the shore. You'll be going out of your way to find this hill but it's more than worth the detour if you're a fan of the steep stuff. Confronted by numerous 'traffic free' signs, I asked the car park attendant if I was allowed to ride down. "Of course," he said, "but you'll not be able to ride back up no matter how fit you are." My eyes narrowed and I raced down to the bottom. Once at the base, engage your largest sprocket and hit the slope, which starts immediately at 20%. It's a dark, rough single carriageway road that offers little to no respite. Where you can have a breather take it, as the higher it gets the harder it gets. As daylight breaks through the tree canopy on the upper slopes, I'd estimate the bends reach nearly 30%. What a road.

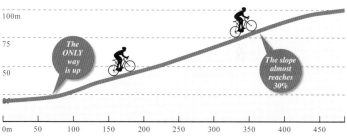

The
ONLY
way
is up

The slope
almost
reaches
30%

## FACTFILE

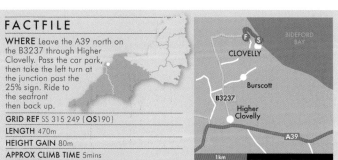

**WHERE** Leave the A39 north on the B3237 through Higher Clovelly. Pass the car park, then take the left turn at the junction past the 25% sign. Ride to the seafront then back up.

**GRID REF** SS 315 249 (OS190)

**LENGTH** 470m

**HEIGHT GAIN** 80m

**APPROX CLIMB TIME** 5mins

# ASHCULME HILL

## ASHCULME, DEVON

The southern flank of the Blackdown Hills is a little less straightforward than the north face: instead of an orderly line of climbs spanning west to east it's more of a tangle of lanes. And in this tangle, if you can find it, is this climb. I could have chosen any number of short and vicious ascents but this one took my fancy and it did not disappoint. Pick your way through the agricultural lanes in the valley, and where you come across a slight clearing you'll see the hill rise up in front of you. This first stretch, between tall hedgerows and across a slightly battered surface, is 25% all the way to the white house on the horizon. Here this savage little road levels before kicking up again, the surface worse but the slope kinder – only just though – up to a second mini break. From here it's just the narrow, twisting finale to the junction at the top, where the legs will insist: ENOUGH.

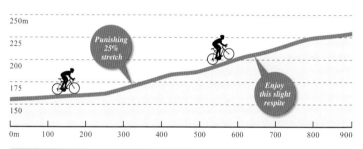

Punishing 25% stretch

Enjoy this slight respite

## FACTFILE

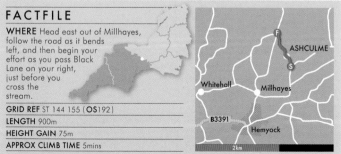

**WHERE** Head east out of Millhayes, follow the road as it bends left, and then begin your effort as you pass Black Lane on your right, just before you cross the stream.

ASHCULME

Whitehall    Millhayes

B3391

Hemyock

2km

**GRID REF** ST 144 155 (OS192)

**LENGTH** 900m

**HEIGHT GAIN** 75m

**APPROX CLIMB TIME** 5mins

# CHINEWAY HILL

OTTERY ST MARY, DEVON

Situated in the official East Devon Area of Outstanding Natural Beauty, the best part of this climb lies at its tail, but as it rises all the way from the centre of Ottery St Mary it would be rude not to document it all. The first two kilometres are very tame, always going upwards but nothing that will stress your legs – that's all ahead, and the first sign of trouble comes when you catch sight of the 20% sign. The ridge above is lined with a row of conifers, a massed army of green staring down at you. This is where the party ends and the serious work starts. The road arcs up to the left past a lone house, not quite 20% but hard enough. Then it heads into the woods, still not quite 20% as it weaves between the trees – in fact to my eye I don't think it ever quite reaches that advertised gradient. Still, that takes nothing away from this beautiful, smooth, winding climb, so push on upwards to finish at the brow opposite the White Cross picnic area.

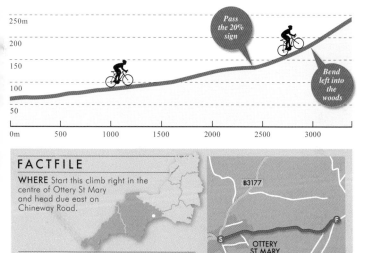

## FACTFILE

**WHERE** Start this climb right in the centre of Ottery St Mary and head due east on Chineway Road.

**GRID REF** SY 131 959 (OS192)

**LENGTH** 3360m

**HEIGHT GAIN** 188m

**APPROX CLIMB TIME** 8.5mins

# RONCOMBE HILL

## COTFORD, DEVON

Not another 33% climb, I hear you cry: oh yes, and this one is a peach! In this part of the world every second road is nasty and steep, so a real killer needs to boast something special – Roncombe Hill has that X factor. Approaching from the west, you begin the climb over a small bridge with the rest of the route clearly in sight. The ferocious-looking slope picks its way skyward up the ridge with little deviation. On the approach to Roncombe Farm, the narrow, debris-covered slope kicks up to 20% before kinking first right then left. Now it's steeper still, and stuck firmly in your bottom gear you'll be firmly in survival mode as you pound the pedals across its rippled and rugged surface. Hitting a maximum of 33% past the kennels, a brow suddenly appears as you bend right, and the hard work is over. Now you can sit down and spin to the finish at the T-junction.

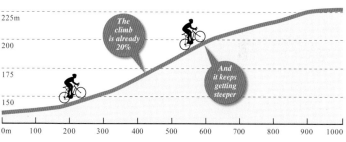

The climb is already 20%

And it keeps getting steeper

## FACTFILE

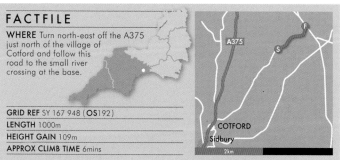

**WHERE** Turn north-east off the A375 just north of the village of Cotford and follow this road to the small river crossing at the base.

| | |
|---|---|
| **GRID REF** SY 167 948 (**OS**192) | |
| **LENGTH** 1000m | |
| **HEIGHT GAIN** 109m | |
| **APPROX CLIMB TIME** 6mins | |

# SALCOMBE HILL

## SIDMOUTH, DEVON

All roads out of Sidmouth head upwards but the two either side of the town are of particular note. Heading west is Peak Hill, used for the 2006 National Hill Climb Championship, while heading east is Salcombe Hill. Peak Hill rises from the seafront, bypassing busy car parks that get extremely crowded in summer, so head for Salcombe Hill. An equally steep ascent, it is perhaps a little shorter, but much quieter. Start on Salcombe Road and climb past the houses lining the steep early slopes heading towards the observatory at the summit. The road soon bends left into thick tree cover. As you climb, so the canopy rises, and soon you're enveloped by giant old trees either side, their branches arching and meeting high above. These murky, quiet and chilly upper slopes reach 20% in some areas but soon slacken off as the road bends right to level out at a car park.

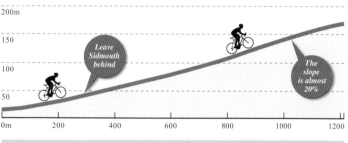

Leave Sidmouth behind

The slope is almost 20%

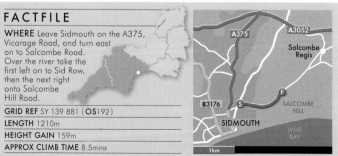

## FACTFILE

**WHERE** Leave Sidmouth on the A375, Vicarage Road, and turn east on to Salcombe Road. Over the river take the first left on to Sid Row, then the next right onto Salcombe Hill Road.

**GRID REF** SY 139 881 (OS192)

**LENGTH** 1210m

**HEIGHT GAIN** 159m

**APPROX CLIMB TIME** 8.5mins

# STOKE HILL

## EXETER, DEVON

There are a couple of ways up Stoke Hill just to the north of Exeter, and this, Pennsylvania Road, is the quietest and so is the one used for races. Following the exit from the A396 it's steep straight away, mostly around 10% but possibly touching 15% in the lead up to the first left-hand corner. After this you're thrust into a right-hand bend where the slope eases slightly. Once you've negotiated these deviations the worst of the gradient is behind you and from now on the climb is significantly kinder on the legs, twisting its way through the woods. As the canopy of branches fades, the surrounding trees are replaced by high hedgerows, which continue to obscure any view. From now on the climbing is never too tough. Pass the entrance to Stoke Woods, go back through some more trees, and then follow the road round to the left where you reach the brow – at last there's a decent vista.

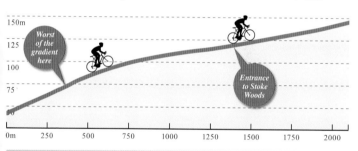

Worst of the gradient here

Entrance to Stoke Woods

## FACTFILE

**WHERE** Travel south from Stoke Canon on the A396 (to the north of Exeter) and take the second left, heading south on Pennsylvania Road.

| | |
|---|---|
| **GRID REF** | SX 923 952 (OS192) |
| **LENGTH** | 2100m |
| **HEIGHT GAIN** | 109m |
| **APPROX CLIMB TIME** | 6 mins |

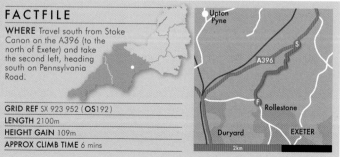

# DOCCOMBE HILL

Begin this climb by rolling over a small stone bridge, then up on to an instantly steep slope. Immediately your muscles will scream NO, but just tell them to shut up, as this initial sharp ramp is over before you know it and the rest of the climb is pure bliss. Once you pass the car park on your left, it is simply brilliant all the way to the village of Doccombe. Twisting through the woods, the perfectly tempered slope flatters your vertical progress proving again that an awesome ascent does not have to rip your legs off. There are a couple of places where the gradient almost vanishes altogether – I was tempted here to engage the big ring but resisted, no need to get carried away. Up through Doccombe, the slope does bite a bit, on its way into the huge, sweeping right-hand bend. It climbs harder and harder as it turns, providing a demanding finish to a glorious road.

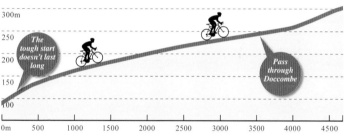

The tough start doesn't last long

Pass through Doccombe

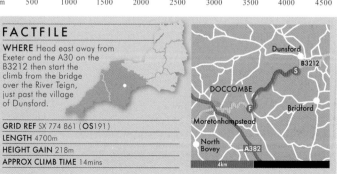

## FACTFILE

**WHERE** Head east away from Exeter and the A30 on the B3212 then start the climb from the bridge over the River Teign, just past the village of Dunsford.

**GRID REF** SX 774 861 (OS191)

**LENGTH** 4700m

**HEIGHT GAIN** 218m

**APPROX CLIMB TIME** 14mins

# OLD GREYSTONE HILL

## MILTON ABBOT, DEVON

Immaculately surfaced and perfectly pitched, this road is just heaven to ride. Heading east away from Launceston along the B3362, you start the climb after crossing Greystone Bridge, where you can take some speed from the hump before bending right. The stiffest slopes are at the base, but they're not too hard and don't last very long. And as the road makes its way up through the woods, if you have good legs, you'll have a number of sprockets spare at the back. You can enjoy climbing at pace here, and once out of the woods the slope eases further, continuing its giant arc left. The altitude gain ceases momentarily with a slight dip past the church at Dunterton where you can ready yourself for the push to the summit. Take some momentum from the downhill to help you reach the approaching left-hand kink, then settle into the long, dead-straight false flat to the summit at the junction where the road bends right.

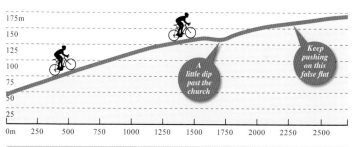

*A little dip past the church*

*Keep pushing on this false flat*

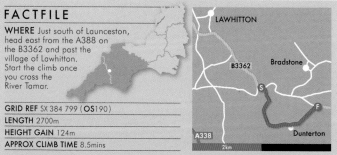

## FACTFILE

**WHERE** Just south of Launceston, head east from the A388 on the B3362 and past the village of Lawhitton. Start the climb once you cross the River Tamar.

**GRID REF** SX 384 799 (OS190)

**LENGTH** 2700m

**HEIGHT GAIN** 124m

**APPROX CLIMB TIME** 8.5mins

# RUNDLESTONE

## TAVISTOCK, DEVON

This climb takes you in stages of varying gradient to the very top of Dartmoor. Beginning with a sharp kick out of Tavistock, the B3357 then eases for a while. Still climbing but only gently, you bump along the rough surface under trees and approach the first portion of pain. Take your momentum on to a silky-smooth section of 15% gradient, climb hard, and then bank right across a cattle grid. Next, veer left – as you reach a brow you will see a TV mast far in the distance: this is your goal. Enjoy the middle section of all but flat road, then drop sharply at Merrivale, bend right, cross the river, and immediately head left and up again. Your legs will hurt as the effort kicks in once more. After a couple of 12% corners you are over the steepest climbing and just the gentle but still not easy upper slopes remain. Eventually you reach the base of the private road that leads to the mast.

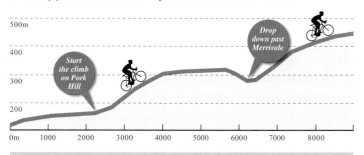

Start the climb on Pork Hill

Drop down past Merrivale

## FACTFILE

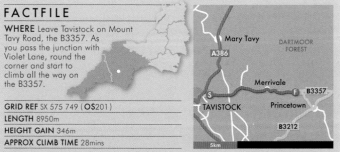

**WHERE** Leave Tavistock on Mount Tavy Road, the B3357. As you pass the junction with Violet Lane, round the corner and start to climb all the way on the B3357.

| | |
|---|---|
| **GRID REF** SX 575 749 (**OS**201) | |
| **LENGTH** 8950m | |
| **HEIGHT GAIN** 346m | |
| **APPROX CLIMB TIME** 28mins | |

# DARTMEET

## DARTMEET, DEVON

Tucked away in the south-east corner of Dartmoor amid a labyrinth of valleys lies the tiny village of Dartmeet, home to Badgers Holt, the place where the east and west tributaries of the River Dart meet. This part of the country is hill-climbing paradise. Cyclists could spend days here and not ride the same hill twice. All the roads are up and down and up and down – there's not an inch of flat – and to top it all they're set in stunning scenery. Spoilt for choice, it's hard to favour one climb over another, but the road away from Badgers Holt and up over Yar Tor is a real killer: 20% from the gun, it takes off up the hillside, twisting slightly left then right with very little deviation in direction or gradient. It's well surfaced and well marked, and there's a couple of kinks before you reach the brow and finish adjacent to a car park surrounded by sheep, cattle, and the famous wild Dartmoor ponies.

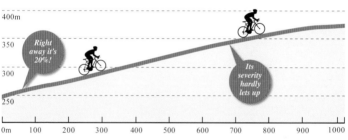

*Right away it's 20%!*

*Its severity hardly lets up*

## FACTFILE

**WHERE** At the end of the B3357 ride through Dartmeet, over the bridge, and past the sign for Badgers Holt. Now heead up on to Yar Tor Down.

**GRID REF** SX 680 732 (OS191)

**LENGTH** 1020m

**HEIGHT GAIN** 119m

**APPROX CLIMB TIME** 6mins

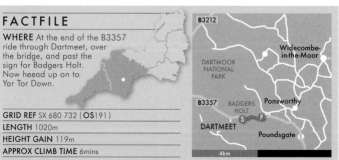

# LADY MEADOW

If you find yourself in Widecombe-in-the-Moor to ride the more famous route out of town (see page 138), you shouldn't leave before also sampling the delights of this road. Tucked away at the bottom of the village, it's equally if not more savage and certainly a lot quieter. The climb starts abruptly as its narrow course winds up between crumbling walls and twisted trees. The next stretch, past a few farmhouses, doesn't present too much of a problem, but the higher you climb the more testing it becomes. Out of the trees, away from the crumbling walls, is where the true beauty of this road presents itself, and where it will put some strain on your legs. The gradient reaches close to 20% and the broken stone walls are replaced by rolling grassland and gorse bushes. As the sky opens the slope relaxes and you can sit back and enjoy the final few metres.

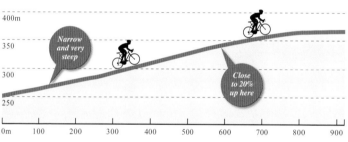

## FACTFILE

**WHERE** Head south out of Widecombe-in-the-Moor and turn right just after the school.

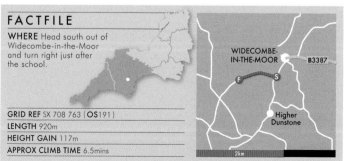

**GRID REF** SX 708 763 (OS191)

**LENGTH** 920m

**HEIGHT GAIN** 117m

**APPROX CLIMB TIME** 6.5mins

RATING
7/10

# WIDECOMBE

## WIDECOMBE-IN-THE-MOOR, DEVON

Being the region's tourist hub, it seems every second building in Widecombe is selling souvenirs of one sort or another. If souvenirs aren't what you are looking for, rather burning legs and puffed-out lungs, then you're in the right place for those too. The climb out of Widecombe is the jewel in Dartmoor's crown: a well-marked and well-surfaced road that conceals little of its challenging nature. Leave the village, cross the East Webburn River, and get stuck into the steep incline. With no corners, just a brief dogleg deviation, the constant, remorseless 1-in-6 gradient doesn't give you a second's respite. The summit is in view almost the whole of the way up to the car park on the exposed Bonehill Down. It was the scene for the 1990 National Hill-Climb Championships and it took the great Chris Boardman just four minutes and ten seconds to conquer. If you can scale it in double that then you'll be doing well.

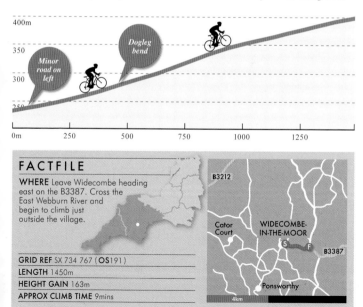

## FACTFILE

**WHERE** Leave Widecombe heading east on the B3387. Cross the East Webburn River and begin to climb just outside the village.

| | |
|---|---|
| **GRID REF** SX 734 767 (**OS**191) | |
| **LENGTH** 1450m | |
| **HEIGHT GAIN** 163m | |
| **APPROX CLIMB TIME** 9mins | |

RATING 5/10

# NEWBRIDGE HILL

## POUNDSGATE, DEVON

Hidden in the interlocking hills on the eastern edge of Dartmoor are numerous arduous roads, and this one is particularly impressive. Start the climb as you roll over the small stone bridge at the base, pass the large car park on your left, and head up into the woods. The gradient gradually creeps up until it becomes quite stiff around the left-hand hairpin, and it continues to test you as you ride out into open land. With views over the valley to your left you then change direction and head north – here is where the climb will hurt the legs. This long, demanding stretch across the rugged moorland is a struggle all the way to the point where another road joins from the left. Once through Poundsgate the gradient increases again and you are faced with over a kilometre of 10% slope up to the splendour of the empty moor and the summit of Dartmeet (see page 134).

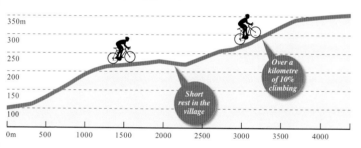

Short rest in the village

Over a kilometre of 10% climbing

## FACTFILE

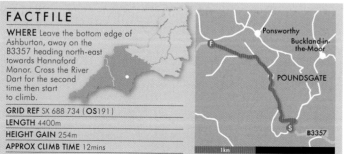

**WHERE** Leave the bottom edge of Ashburton, away on the B3357 heading north-east towards Hannaford Manor. Cross the River Dart for the second time then start to climb.

**GRID REF** SX 688 734 (OS191)

**LENGTH** 4400m

**HEIGHT GAIN** 254m

**APPROX CLIMB TIME** 12mins

Ponsworthy
Buckland-in-the-Moor
POUNDSGATE
B3357
1km

# HAYTOR

## BOVEY TRACEY, DEVON

Rising up the eastern side of Dartmoor is the long climb to Haytor Rocks. Beginning just outside Bovey Tracey, the B3387 forks left at Five Wyches Cross. Rising up to 12%, the rough lower slopes are by and large tree-covered, but as you pass the Edgemoor Hotel you emerge from under the protection of the woods. Here the gradient steadies, although not enough for you to relax. Ullacombe Farm signals the end of the easier stuff and the road bends left, passing over a cattle grid and rising steeply into the national park. It's really hard going through a small wooded section and then it eases once more before the hardest stretch. A long, tough grind brings you out on to open moorland, where you climb gently towards and past the Haytor Visitor Centre – the base for walkers and climbers visiting the giant granite outcrop that towers above your final strength-sapping push to the summit.

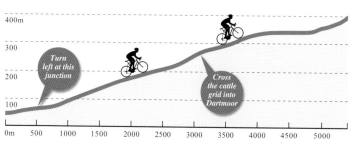

Turn left at this junction

Cross the cattle grid into Dartmoor

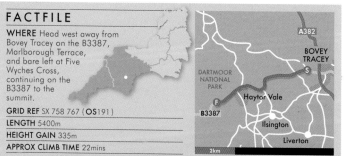

## FACTFILE

**WHERE** Head west away from Bovey Tracey on the B3387, Marlborough Terrace, and bare left at Five Wyches Cross, continuing on the B3387 to the summit.

**GRID REF** SX 758 767 (OS191)

**LENGTH** 5400m

**HEIGHT GAIN** 335m

**APPROX CLIMB TIME** 22mins

RATING
6/10

# COOMBE HILL

## COOMBE, CORNWALL

At the top of this climb sits the vast GCHQ complex. Surrounded by multiple levels of fencing, you can't help but feel you're being watched as you approach it, gasping for air, on your journey to the summit of Coombe Hill. Like so many of the roads that line the west Cornish coast this one first plunges down into the valley before rising rapidly back out, although that's not a description of the speed at which you'll be travelling. Any stored momentum from the descent will soon evaporate as you pass the 15% sign, which is a lie, as it's easily 25% round the first tight corner. Grind up through the trees to reach a wonderful hairpin with views over the sea ahead and then bend right to weave between tall, neat hedgerows. From here the slope eases significantly. As the radar dishes come into view on the horizon you line up for the final demanding ramp to the summit, which sits at the entrance to the secretive facility.

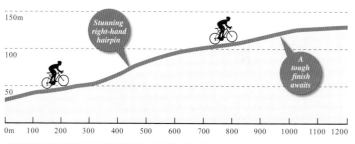

Stunning right-hand hairpin

A tough finish awaits

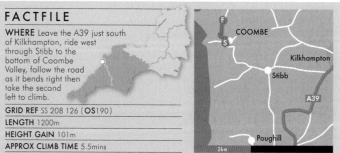

## FACTFILE

**WHERE** Leave the A39 just south of Kilkhampton, ride west through Stibb to the bottom of Coombe Valley, follow the road as it bends right then take the second left to climb.

**GRID REF** SS 208 126 (OS190)

**LENGTH** 1200m

**HEIGHT GAIN** 101m

**APPROX CLIMB TIME** 5.5mins

RATING 7/10

# CRACKINGTON HAVEN

## CRACKINGTON HAVEN, CORNWALL

Although not quite as savage as its close neighbour Millook, this is another classic Cornish coastal climb. In fact, there are three brutal ascents from the base in the tiny fishing village of Crackington Haven – one heading up to Middle Crackington, the punishing route out towards Wainhouse Corner, and this one, the climb that follows the coast south. Starting from the shore, ride south out of the village then take a right-hand turn past the sign warning of gates. There's a brief lull and then the gradient kicks in, and it just gets steeper and steeper. Twisting upwards and heading due south, you pick your way along the cliff side between the high hedgerows with the sound of waves crashing below, fading with each pedal stroke. There's a brace of 20% sections to tackle, then, with most of the hard work done, a brief dip before the final stretch to the finish adjacent to a farm, high above the coast.

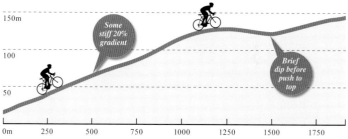

_Some stiff 20% gradient_

_Brief dip before push to top_

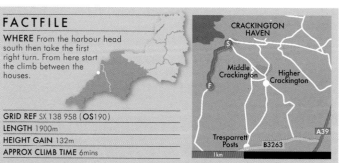

## FACTFILE

**WHERE** From the harbour head south then take the first right turn. From here start the climb between the houses.

**GRID REF** SX 138 958 (**OS**190)

**LENGTH** 1900m

**HEIGHT GAIN** 132m

**APPROX CLIMB TIME** 6mins

# MILLOOK

## MILLOOK, CORNWALL

I couldn't wait to ride this climb. Any road rated 30% gets my pulse racing and I felt like a kid on my way to Disneyland as I rode south from Bude. Upon arrival I discovered not one, but two 30% ascents. Which would I choose for the book? I could pick only one, so I chose the route south. Although it lacks the dramatic final corner of the route north it is, all things considered, the tougher challenge. Bending left away from the bridge at the base, you're almost instantly faced with a 30% corner, but what follows is worse. You are led into a remorseless stretch of 20% climbing. You'll be at your maximum and need to recover, but it's just not possible. On and on it goes, steeper still in the corners. It is now just about survival. Although easing slightly in places, the final rise will take everything you've got. Keep your focus on the brow, reach this and, although it's not quite the top, you're safe and can finally relax.

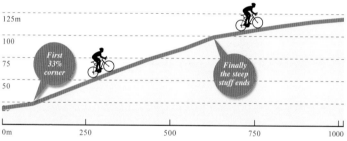

First 33% corner

Finally the steep stuff ends

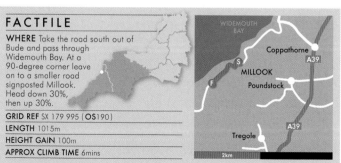

## FACTFILE

**WHERE** Take the road south out of Bude and pass through Widemouth Bay. At a 90-degree corner leave on to a smaller road signposted Millook. Head down 30%, then up 30%.

**GRID REF** SX 179 995 (OS190)

**LENGTH** 1015m

**HEIGHT GAIN** 100m

**APPROX CLIMB TIME** 6mins

RATING
5/10

# BOSCASTLE HILL

## BOSCASTLE, CORNWALL

To ride this climb you'll first have to descend one of the three routes into Boscastle, heading all the way to the harbour's edge before turning round to rise back out. Starting from sea level, head west on New Road, climb sharply to the hairpin, and then continue on the 9-10% slope, which runs level with the second storey of a row of houses on your left. The smooth, narrow path picks its way up to a large, sweeping corner where you leave New Road to head left on to Doctors Hill. Here the gradient eases by a percentage point. Inching upwards through the trees, kinking left and right, it's a significant amount of time before you reach the first of two pronounced bends where you can catch a glimpse of the ocean far below. You've already climbed a fair height but it's far from over, as exiting the second corner you must rise on and on to eventually summit at the staggered meeting point of four roads.

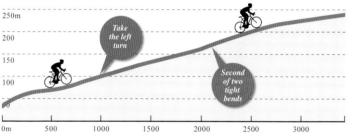

## FACTFILE

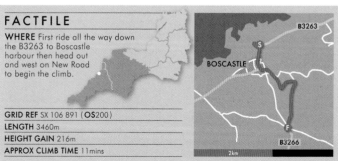

**WHERE** First ride all the way down the B3263 to Boscastle harbour then head out and west on New Road to begin the climb.

| | |
|---|---|
| **GRID REF** SX 106 891 (**OS**200) | |
| **LENGTH** 3460m | |
| **HEIGHT GAIN** 216m | |
| **APPROX CLIMB TIME** 11mins | |

# BODMIN EAST MOOR

## TREBARTHA, CORNWALL

This climb takes a while to really get going. Take the first left after Trebartha –
the road rolls up and down for a while, so if you're looking to post a time on
social media, it's important to know where the climb really begins. You'll find the
true base in a small gully bisecting a group of farmhouses – from there the climb
rises rapidly up on a solid gradient. The first third of the ascent is a real battle
through the woods, with a handful of kinks and bends on the narrow road between
the crumbling stone walls. After a brace of false summits the gradient abates and
from here on progress to the top is much easier. At first you continue through the
trees but then once over a cattle grid the sky opens up and you head into the heart
of Bodmin Moor. Up ahead the brow is constantly in view: click down a couple
of gears and sprint past the gorse bushes to finish in beautiful open landscape.

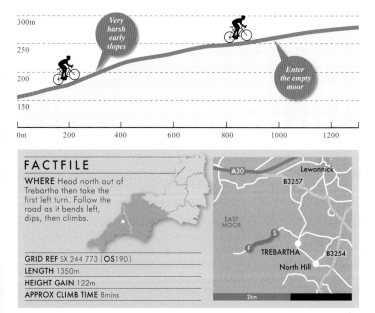

## FACTFILE

**WHERE** Head north out of
Trebartha then take the
first left turn. Follow the
road as it bends left,
dips, then climbs.

| | |
|---|---|
| **GRID REF** SX 244 773 (OS190) | |
| **LENGTH** 1350m | |
| **HEIGHT GAIN** 122m | |
| **APPROX CLIMB TIME** 8mins | |

# CARADON HILL

## MINIONS, CORNWALL

Due to the global phenomenon of a certain animation franchise, the village of Minions isn't quite as sleepy as it once was. Unless you've been living in a box for the past few years you'll be well aware of the little blue and yellow characters, and they are all over this village. But we aren't here for Minions, we're here for this awesome climb, although the portion that leaves the village isn't the whole story, just the icing on the cake. You will need to climb a significant distance to reach Minions first and I recommend you take the route from Upton Cross in the north, covering two kilometres at an average gradient of 6%, which will prime the legs for the finale. As you turn past the post office, there's a long gentle approach, then the slope violently ramps up. Here you begin the glorious ride up this solitary hill to the aerials at its summit and stunning, uninterrupted views in all directions.

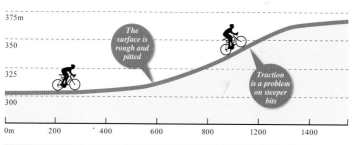

The surface is rough and pitted

Traction is a problem on steeper bits

## FACTFILE

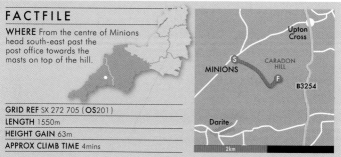

**WHERE** From the centre of Minions head south-east past the post office towards the masts on top of the hill.

**GRID REF** SX 272 705 (OS201)

**LENGTH** 1550m

**HEIGHT GAIN** 63m

**APPROX CLIMB TIME** 4mins

# KIT HILL

## CALLINGTON, CORNWALL

What an incredible place Kit Hill is – perched high above the surrounding countryside, this is simply a must-ride climb. To make the most of it, start in the village of Luckett, just inside the Cornish border, as you cross the small stream. The lower slopes are brutal, 20% for what seems like an age, then they ease slightly before slamming back into more 20% through the woods. Once free of the trees the pitch relaxes just a touch, but not enough to make it comfortable – your only chance of respite comes at the junction with the B3257. Here you can briefly pause before launching into another nasty 20% ramp. After a brief level a right turn sets you up for the summit. The road is now rough and punctuated by rudimentary speed bumps that will hinder your progress. However the views in all directions are simply outstanding, making the toil well worth it. Bend round to the left to finish in the shadow of the old mine chimney.

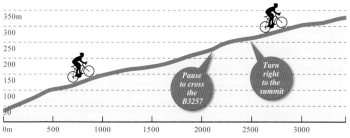

*Pause to cross the B3257*

*Turn right to the summit*

## FACTFILE

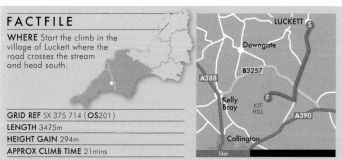

**WHERE** Start the climb in the village of Luckett where the road crosses the stream and head south.

**GRID REF** SX 375 714 (**OS**201)

**LENGTH** 3475m

**HEIGHT GAIN** 294m

**APPROX CLIMB TIME** 21mins

# BISHOP'S WOOD

## BURLAWN, CORNWALL

Hidden in a dark labyrinth of narrow, twisting lanes south of Wadebridge lies the climb of Bishop's Wood. It's remarkably easy to get lost around here; the lack of landmarks in the shadowy lanes can easily disorientate you. You will finally find the base in thick woodland, but I'm betting by the time you reach the top you'll wish you hadn't. Start as you cross the stream then round the bend, pass the first 28% warning sign, and keep left at the fork. If you can climb this next stretch of road you'll pretty much be able to climb anything. Viciously steep, strewn with gravel and debris, punctuated by momentum-sapping ridges, it's a perfect storm of obstacles. A large lump in the tarmac marks the end of the steepest stretch. It's still very hard after this, 20%; it then eases back before hitting 20% again. It does eventually abate and after numerous kinks right and left, you'll reach the summit of Cornwall's hidden beast.

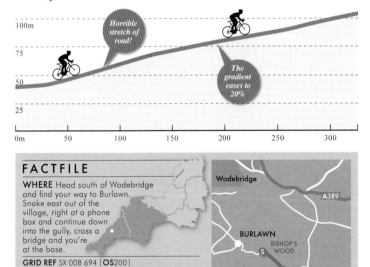

Horrible stretch of road?

The gradient eases to 20%

100m
75
50
25
0m    50    100    150    200    250    300

## FACTFILE

**WHERE** Head south of Wadebridge and find your way to Burlawn. Snake east out of the village, right at a phone box and continue down into the gully, cross a bridge and you're at the base.

**GRID REF** SX 008 694 (OS200)

**LENGTH** 325m

**HEIGHT GAIN** 47m

**APPROX CLIMB TIME** 5mins

Wadebridge

A389

BURLAWN

BISHOP'S WOOD

S

F

1km

# DULOE HILL

## DULOE, CORNWALL

On my way to the base of this climb I swear I didn't ride a road wide enough for a single car, or a road that wasn't covered in mud and other debris. It was a relief then to find this to be clean, smooth, generously wide, and just wonderful to climb. Begin by cresting the small bridge over the railway line and take a little momentum into the demanding early slopes. The first third is hard work, snaking this way and that through the woods up to a slight dip, followed by what looks like level ground. With this change in gradient I switched up to the big ring, but then instantly started to suffer so changed my mind and clicked back down again – it's not quite as flat as it looks. Following this, the slope increases in pitch once more, forcing you to put in more effort up past the entrance to Duloe Manor. Up ahead a road joins from the left; keep heading right to finish just past the village sign.

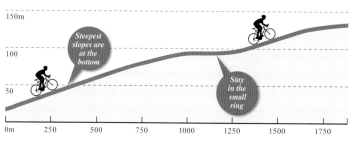

Steepest slopes are at the bottom

Stay in the small ring

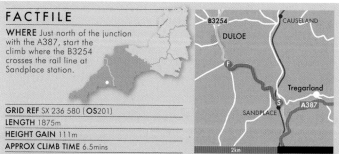

## FACTFILE

**WHERE** Just north of the junction with the A387, start the climb where the B3254 crosses the rail line at Sandplace station.

**GRID REF** SX 236 580 (OS201)

**LENGTH** 1875m

**HEIGHT GAIN** 111m

**APPROX CLIMB TIME** 6.5mins

# TALLAND HILL

## POLPERRO, CORNWALL

Bold 'no entry' signs greet you at the base. Obviously these are intended to halt those with motor vehicles, as no one would attempt to ride up Talland Hill on a bike, would they? The joy this road offers those in search of the nation's toughest gradients is matched only by the beauty of the Cornish fishing village at its base. There's scant room for a run-up amid the tourists, but get what you can, stick it in your biggest sprocket, and attack. Not since I ascended Hardknott and Wrynose have I been forced to ride such a distance out of the saddle, but still, it's worth it. Through the neatly painted houses on either side, it's all but dead straight and doesn't back off an inch until you reach the wooded area halfway up. Pass the turn for the primary school and push on through the final gentle climbing that levels just before the T-junction. Turn left here and head back down into town to ride it again – it's impossible not to, it's that good.

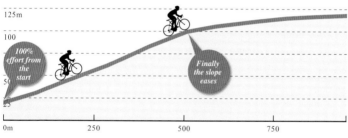

125m

100

100% effort from the start

Finally the slope eases

50

25

0m          250          500          750

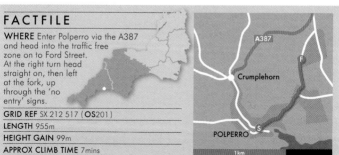

## FACTFILE

**WHERE** Enter Polperro via the A387 and head into the traffic free zone on to Ford Street. At the right turn head straight on, then left at the fork, up through the 'no entry' signs.

**GRID REF** SX 212 517 (**OS**201)

**LENGTH** 955m

**HEIGHT GAIN** 99m

**APPROX CLIMB TIME** 7mins

A387

Crumplehorn

F

S

POLPERRO

1km

# GROVE ROAD

## ST MAWES, CORNWALL

No matter where the 30% gradient signs are hidden, I will find them, and this one is certainly well concealed. St Mawes doesn't get much passing trade as it lies at the end of a peninsula with just one way in or out, unless you arrive by boat. I dropped down into town on the main road and made my way round the beautiful harbour, looking for the tiny road that rises between two buildings to form the start of this vicious climb. Bending right, Commercial Street soon becomes Grove Road, which then bends left into a wall of tarmac. Engage your lowest gear and fight the savage 30% slope through the slight kinks in direction all the way to the white house ahead. Passing this landmark, the task becomes slightly easier and you'll be able to change down a few gears, but don't go too far because the final few hundred metres are slightly steeper to the junction with the main road.

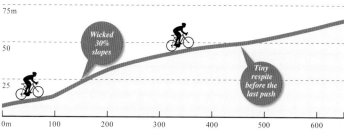

75m

Wicked 30% slopes

50

Tiny respite before the last push

25

0m    100    200    300    400    500    600

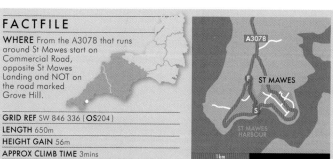

## FACTFILE

**WHERE** From the A3078 that runs around St Mawes start on Commercial Road, opposite St Mawes Landing and NOT on the road marked Grove Hill.

**GRID REF** SW 846 336 (**OS204**)

**LENGTH** 650m

**HEIGHT GAIN** 56m

**APPROX CLIMB TIME** 3mins

A3078

**ST MAWES**

F

S

ST MAWES HARBOUR

1km

RATING
7/10

# BLUE HILLS

## ST AGNES, CORNWALL

If you make the effort to find the Blue Hills tucked away to the north of St Agnes, you must make sure you ride up them both before moving on. The twin ascents rising up either side of the valley are both wild beasts waiting to tear into your legs, but it's the southern flank that I'll focus on, and for one good reason – its first bend. As you can see from the photograph opposite it's nearly vertical, and about as steep as any bend I've come across in the UK. Luckily there's a good line of sight up the road, so you can ride wide on the right-hand side to lessen lesson the impact of its 33% apex. Once round, the slope settles into a punishing ramp of 20-25% gradient, picking its way precariously up the side of the steep bank. As the road begins to veer right the slope abates, but does not really let go until you have the village in sight. If you haven't already ridden the other side, turn round and head back down.

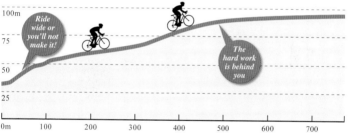

*Ride wide or you'll not make it!*

*The hard work is behind you*

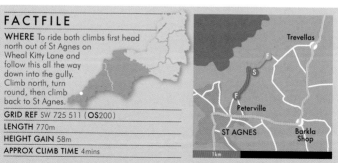

## FACTFILE

**WHERE** To ride both climbs first head north out of St Agnes on Wheal Kitty Lane and follow this all the way down into the gully. Climb north, turn round, then climb back to St Agnes.

**GRID REF** SW 725 511 (OS200)

**LENGTH** 770m

**HEIGHT GAIN** 58m

**APPROX CLIMB TIME** 4mins

Trevallas

Peterville

ST AGNES

Barkla Shop

1km

# PORTHMEOR HILL

## ST IVES, CORNWALL

As I sat on the sand eating my fish and chips, I soon realised that it wasn't just me who'd struggled up this climb. Every vehicle that passed me along the seafront put in a distinct burst of speed as soon as it came to the base to carry it round the bottom bend and up past the graveyard. From large vans clunking down the gears to scooters revving their engines to shreds, no one was finding Porthmeor Hill easy, and it isn't. The start is abrupt: you bend left away from the beach and instantly the slope reaches close to 20%. This torment continues for close to 200 metres, all the way to the right-hand bend on the horizon ahead. Once you've changed direction the slope eases, allowing you to get your breath back for the third part of the climb. The finale is tough again, not as gruelling as the opening stretch but still very hard, twisting between houses before eventually leading you to the summit.

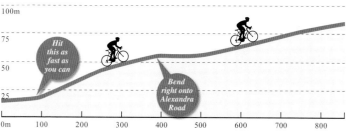

Hit this as fast as you can

Bend right onto Alexandra Road

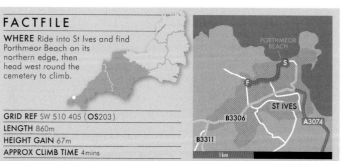

## FACTFILE

**WHERE** Ride into St Ives and find Porthmeor Beach on its northern edge, then head west round the cemetery to climb.

**GRID REF** SW 510 405 (OS203)

**LENGTH** 860m

**HEIGHT GAIN** 67m

**APPROX CLIMB TIME** 4mins

# RIDE THEM ALL

## GO ON, I DARE YOU!

Many of the climbs on this checklist come in small clusters, huddled together in the various areas of high ground that define the region. From the Cotsworlds to the Mendips, the Blackdown Hills to the Quantocks and of course Exmoor and Dartmoor, if you find a convenient base you could easily conquer five or more in a single ride. If you've already been filling in the checklists in the original *100 Greatest Cycling Climbs* and its sequel, *Another 100 Greatest Cycling Climbs*, then you can transfer those ticks across to see what gaps are left, and which hills you still need to bag before you can say you've ridden them all!

## GLOUCESTERSHIRE AND WILTSHIRE

| Hill | Date Ridden | Time |
|------|-------------|------|
| Dover's Hill | | |
| Saintbury | | |
| Salter's Lane | | |
| Bushcombe Lane | | |
| Birdlip Hill | | |
| Haresfield Beacon | | |
| Frocester Hill | | |
| Symonds Yat | | |
| Bear Hill | | |
| Oakridge Lynch | | |
| Owlpen Hill | | |
| The Broadway | | |
| Hackpen Hill | | |
| Milton Hill | | |
| Bowden Hill | | |
| Redhorn Hill | | |
| Westbury Hill | | |
| Park Hill | | |
| Fovant Downs | | |

## SOMERSET AND DORSET

| Hill | Date Ridden | Time |
|------|-------------|------|
| Belmont Hill | | |
| Vale Street | | |
| Weston Hill | | |
| Bannerdown Road | | |
| Prospect Place | | |
| Shaft Road | | |
| Burrington Combe | | |
| Cheddar Gorge | | |
| Draycott Steep | | |
| Crowcome Combe | | |
| Cothelstone Hill | | |
| Ford Street | | |
| Corfe Hill | | |
| Dunkery Beacon | | |
| Porlock | | |
| Porlock Toll Road | | |
| Gold Hill | | |
| Zig Zag Hill | | |
| Woolland Hill | | |
| Piddle Lane | | |
| White Way | | |
| Portesham Hill | | |
| Grange Hill | | |

## DEVON AND CORNWALL

| Hill | Date Ridden | Time |
|------|-------------|------|
| Countisbury Hill | | |
| Exmoor Forest | | |

| | | |
|---|---|---|
| Trentishoe Down | | |
| Martinhoe Common | | |
| Grasspark Hill | | |
| Challacombe | | |
| Clovelly | | |
| Ashculme Hill | | |
| Chineway Hill | | |
| Roncombe Hill | | |
| Salcombe Hill | | |
| Stoke Hill | | |
| Doccombe Hill | | |
| Old Greystone Hill | | |
| Rundlestone | | |
| Dartmeet | | |
| Lady Meadow | | |
| Widecombe | | |
| Newbridge Hill | | |
| Haytor | | |
| Coombe Hill | | |
| Crackington Haven | | |
| Millook | | |
| Boscastle Hill | | |
| Bodmin East Moor | | |
| Caradon Hill | | |
| Kit Hill | | |
| Bishop's Wood | | |
| Duloe Hill | | |
| Talland Hill | | |
| Grove Road | | |
| Blue Hills | | |
| Porthmeor Hill | | |

Ride them all.

# BRITISH
# CLIMBING
# GUIDES
# ALREADY
# AVAILABLE